FREE CASH GRANTS

Volume I

Scholarships, Business, and Medical Grants

By

Rebecca Harris

Published by
Clarendon House, Inc.

Copyright © 1998 by Clarendon House, Inc.

Second edition.

Researchers: Angela Carr, Ann Marcus, Annette Selver, Connie Wilson, Margaret Smith, Laura Nelson, Susan Lansing, Scott Ward, Gabrielle Potts, Jessie Carson, Willy Potts, Doreen Elm, Tim Greenwood, Ruth Morton, Robert Spence, George Wild, Sue Phillips.

ISBN: 1-886-908-13-3

Printed in the United States of America

Acknowledgments

We would like to take this opportunity to thank the many professionals involved in the development and publication of *Free Cash Grants Volume 1*. A special thank you goes to our support staff and to the federal, state, and private grantmaking organizations all across the country who took the time to share their stories and expertise with us. Most of all, we would like to thank the dedicated individuals who have paved the way by winning free cash grants for their education, business, and medical needs. These creative people are an inspiration to everyone who follows in their footsteps!

A Note from the Publisher

We have made every effort to ensure the accuracy of the information in this book. However, we cannot be held responsible for any errors that may have inadvertently been made, or for changes in any of the information since we went to print. This book is designed to provide information about free cash grants, and is sold with the understanding that the author and publisher are not in any way engaged in or offering accounting, marketing, legal, or any other professional services. In all such matters we recommend that you seek the services of a competent professional. Please always bear in mind that our sole purpose in writing this book is to inform and help you, the reader.

Table of Contents

Overview and Fast Start

This book has been created to make it easy for you to find free cash grants for your education, business, and medical needs. Below you will find a brief summary of the chapters in this book and their contents. Use this book along with the grant listings in *Free Cash Grants Vol. 2* to find the grants that best suit your needs. With the Clarendon Grants Program, you'll have access to the best sources of grants in the country to help you to a better life!

There are three sections in *Free Cash Grants Vol. 1*: Education, Business, and Medical. The Education Section begins with **Chapter 1, There's Money Out There For You!** In this chapter you'll learn why no one should feel they can't attend college because of lack of funds. There is just too much grant and loan money out there for you to think that way!

In **Chapter 2, Planning for Parents**, parents of future college students will learn about all kinds of tips and tricks to make it easy to pay for your child's college education. In **Chapter 3, Planning for Students**, we help students get an idea of what they can do during their high school years to best prepare themselves for college.

Chapter 4, Sailing Through The Application Process, takes the mystery out of filling out applications, taking the SAT and the ACT, and writing personal essays for college applications. Then it's on to **Chapter 5, Federal Financial Aid**, for a look at the programs of the nation's biggest supplier of aid for college: the Federal government.

The next few chapters take you on a tour through even more sources of grants and loans for education. **Chapter 6, Military Programs**, explores the ROTC, military academies, Merchant Marines, National Guard, programs for veterans, and more—programs that can pay up to 100% of your college expenses, plus give you spending money on the side!

In **Chapter 7, Athletic Scholarships**, you'll discover that you don't need to be a star athlete to qualify. Finally, in **Chapter 8, Other Sources of Financial Aid**, you'll read about state programs, private foundations, college programs, AmeriCorps, and Upward Bound. Use the sample letters in this chapter to approach the agencies and organizations that give scholarships for education.

The Business Section has a wealth of information for small business owners seeking grants and loans to start up or expand their operations. **Chapter 9, Getting Ready for Success**, describes what it takes to start your own business and how to prepare yourself to write a business plan. **Chapter 10, All About the SBA**, covers the basics of approaching this very important agency that made over $7.4 BILLION in grants and loans to small businesses last year. **Chapter 11, Federal and State Funding Sources**, presents sources of aid, as does **Chapter 12, Venture Capital Sources. Chapter 13** wraps up the business section with tips on how to **Make Your Business a Winner!**

Next, it's on to the Medical section, where you'll learn about the incredible financial resources available to people with every type of illness and disability. **Chapter 14, Free Cash Grants For Health Care**, has a complete guide on how to get started. **Chapter 15, Self-Help Groups**, has a list of self-help resources nationwide. In **Chapter 16, Veterans Health Benefits**, you'll learn about programs that have the potential to help 1/3 of all Americans. **Chapter 17, The Viatical Option**, describes how people with terminal illnesses can cash out their life insurance policies while they're still alive. And in **Chapter 18, Service Organizations and Foundations**, you'll find many more resources for FREE help for medical needs.

Use this book along with Free Cash Grants, Vol. 2, which has over 2,000 listings of scholarships, grants, and loans for education, business, and medical purposes. The two books work together to give you the best information and resources for obtaining free cash grants available! If you have any questions or need additional assistance, don't hesitate to call the Clarendon Customer Assistance Group at 1-800-258-3770 Monday through Friday between the hours of 5 am and 6 pm PST (or Saturdays 7 am - 1 pm PST).

The final word is, free cash grants are out there just waiting to be claimed. It's up to you to go out and get 'em!

Chapter 1
There's Money Out There
For You!

D o you think you can't go to college because you can't afford it? <u>Nothing could be further from the truth!</u> There are countless avenues of financial assistance available to you, and that's what this book is all about.

<u>Absolutely no student who wants to go to college should be discouraged from going because of the cost.</u> In this day and age, a college education is the key to your earning power for the rest of your life. It's estimated that people with a college education will make a minimum of $600,000 more in their lifetime than those who only graduated from high school. The costs of college are a small price to pay to generate that kind of earning power!

And that's just the financial incentive. With the information superhighway making vast amounts of information available to anyone with a computer, those who know what to do with that information are light years ahead of those who don't. <u>Don't be left behind.</u> The Internet and World Wide Web are quickly creating a culture of people who dominate the job market when it comes to earning power and job security. And those people have a college education.

Finances can be a concern, there is no doubt. The costs of a college education can appear astronomical. Even the least expensive four-year universities can run $10,000 per year, and costs go up from there. Parents may be completely overwhelmed by the costs of tuition alone, not to mention books, fees, and housing.

But rest assured, there is ALWAYS a way. A college education is simply too valuable to pass up just because you think you can't pay for it. The good news is, you don't have to! There are a multitude of government agencies and private foundations with grants, scholarships and loans that make it possible for virtually any student to attend college. <u>In fact, more than 7 million college students receive financial aid each year!</u>

Scholarships are for EVERYONE

You don't have to be a minority, or a straight-A student, or come from a poor family to get scholarships, grants, and loans for your education. <u>On the contrary, ANY student who has the ambition to look for money to pay for college WILL find it.</u> In fact, because of increasing college costs these days, 76% of all students entering college apply for some type of financial aid. That's up 10% from just 10 years ago. The good news is that 10 years ago there was $28 billion available in financial aid from federal, state, and private sources. <u>Today, a record $50 billion is available.</u>

Putting together your college financing is not an endeavor that is free from effort, however. Wading through the financial aid options, filling out forms, and keeping track of deadlines, all takes some work on your part. In this chapter, we'll help you get organized. We'll help you understand the options you face. We'll set out the basics. We'll help you decide which options are best for you. And then we'll show you how to pursue those options.

Types of Aid

Most students find that a combination of money from different financial aid sources works best. This means combining whatever money you can get from your family or your own savings with money from several different grants, scholarships and work-study programs. Remember, don't choose just one type of financial aid or the other. Diversify! Choose from the following types of financial aid.

• **Grants and Scholarships.** This is FREE money. You never have to pay it back. Of course, the money does come with certain conditions. You have to keep up your grades and complete your course of study. Grants are usually blocks of money given to help defray general costs, while scholarships are usually a reduction or waiver of tuition and/or housing fees.

• **Work-Study.** Work-study is often offered along with a grant or scholarship. Students may be offered work on campus by the school's financial aid office, or work in the community through the Federal Work-Study program. Some private foundations also offer work-study programs.

• **Student Loans.** Loans are easier to qualify for than grants or scholarships. But the money must be paid back after college, usually at a fairly low interest rate. Federal student loans are the most common. They often form the backbone of a student's financial package.

Overview: Need-Based Financial Aid

Financial aid can be broken down into need-based aid and merit-based aid. First, we will discuss need-based aid.

A vast majority of the finanical aid that is awarded to students each year is given to families who don't have the money to pay for their child's education. This is need-based aid. Almost 90% of the money that is given to students each year takes the form of need-based scholarships and grants.

<u>You should know that about 90% of need-based financial aid is awarded by the federal government.</u> For this reason, most students begin their quest for financial aid by applying for federal help.

A good general litmus test for seeing if you will qualify for federal need-based financial aid is to get out the family tax return. Check to see if your family made more than $80,000 in one year. If they did, you probably

won't be eligible for federal aid. But don't worry. Students who aren't eligible for federal aid can often get money from private sources—or, they get grants based on academic merit, or other specific skills and interests.

The Mighty FAFSA

Students who are serious about applying for federal need-based aid should request the Free Application for Federal Student Aid, or FAFSA, as soon as possible. This document is the backbone of federal student aid offerings. You will hear a lot about it in this book. This form must be filed in the spring of the year you plan to enter college. Students and parents fill out the form together. The FAFSA gives the federal government a look at your family's ability to pay for college, as well as the projected costs of college. If there is a discrepancy between the two, the federal government jumps in to help.

You can get the FAFSA form by calling the Federal Student Aid Information Center toll free at 1-800-433-3243. Operators are available Monday through Friday from 9 a.m. to 5:30 p.m. EST.

The FAFSA form includes a chart which families can use to figure out whether they are eligible for financial aid from the federal goverment. The chart can also help you figure out how much aid you might get, taking into account your family's assets and income before taxes, as well as the size of your family.

Insider's Tip:

The Federal Student Aid Information Center can also help you find out more about state financial aid (over $1 billion per year), plus private grants and scholarships that focus on your individual needs. For more information call 1-800-433-3243.

The Student Aid Report (SAR)

Six weeks after you have sent in your FAFSA form, you will receive your Student Aid Report (SAR). Read this form carefully. It contains information about how much aid you can expect to receive. You will need to send a copy of Part I of the SAR to the financial aid office of each college to which you've applied. Each college that accepts you will use the FAFSA information to create a financial aid package for you. This package may include aid from one or more sources, including federal, state, college and private sources.

How the FAFSA Works

Here's how the FAFSA determines how much money in financial aid you're eligible for:

• **Parent's Income:**

The parental income figure used to figure eligibility is the taxable and non-taxable income from the year just preceding the year the student will enter college. For instance, parents would use their 1997 tax return for the school year 1998-99. From that, an allowance for food, rent, transportation and laundry is subtracted. For a family of four, that allowance is about $17,000. The allowance increases with the size of the family. Income taxes and employment expense allowances of up to $2,500 may also be deducted, if both parents work. What remains is called available income. Depending on the size of this amount, it is multiplied by a percentage figure of between 25% and 47%. The percentage goes up with the size of the income.

• **Parent's Assets**

Families whose income is less than $50,000 and who are eligible to file a 1040A or 1040 EZ form don't have to include their assets. For others, the assets figure includes the total value of all stocks, bonds, savings accounts and business assets as of the date you sign the FAFSA form. A nest egg allowance is subracted from this. For students whose older parent is at least 47, that allowance is a generous $40,000. The older the parent, the bigger the allowance. What remains is multiped by 5.6%.

• **Student Income**

Students are expected to contribute half of everything that they make, minus what they pay in taxes. They may be allowed to subtract an income protection allowance of $1,750.

• **Student Assets**

35% of a students total assets is expected to be used for college expenses.

• **The Grand Total**

Uncle Sam totals the four figures described above. That becomes the total amount that the family is expected to pay each year toward the child's education. The discrepancy between that and the total costs of the education are what the government tries to make up for in need-based financial aid.

Special Circumstances

When filling out the FAFSA form, parents should be sure to include any special circumstances that will affect the family's financial picture. Don't fail to write these circumstances down. It's important to reveal your entire financial picture, not just the numbers. Here are some special circumstances that could affect your financial outlook and your ability to pay for college:

• A parent who will retire while their son or daughter is in college

• One of the student's parents is deceased

• Parents are paying child care expenses

• Loss of alimony payment once the child has left the house

• Health insurance may not cover the student is in college. What will the additional costs to cover the student be?

• Parents or the student may have unusually high medical or dental costs

• Unusual expenses for the student related to a disability, or expensive supplies, such as for art students

The PROFILE System

Parents and students should know that many colleges do not use the FAFSA system. About 400 private colleges in the United States use another financial aid system known as PROFILE. Some people believe that this method more accurately "profiles" the financial status of the student's family.

For instance, PROFILE includes equity in the family home as an asset, where FAFSA does not. PROFILE also expects the student to contribute to their own education through, at the very least, money brought in through a summer job. In general, PROFILE is more rigorous than FAFSA, and can often mean less financial aid for the student.

Before applying for financial aid, find out whether the colleges you want to attend use the FAFSA or PROFILE systems of financial aid. Call this number to get more information about PROFILE: (609) 771-7725.

Insider's Tip:

Always apply for financial aid as soon as you hear about a scholarship or grant. The earlier, the better! For Federal aid, this means filing the FAFSA form as soon after January 1 as possible.

Bargaining for More Aid

After you get word from the colleges you applied to on how much aid is available, you are free to choose the college you want to attend. Most students base this decision on how much financial aid a particular college offers. Colleges are very aware of this fact, and for this reason, bargaining for more financial aid is definitely an option. If you aren't happy with the amount of financial aid that has been offered by the college, you are perfectly within your rights to call the college's financial aid office and ask for more.

Have your parents do the calling. Your parents can even use a good offer from one college to force the college you REALLY want to attend into giving you a better financial aid package.

Be aware that each college's way of responding to requests for more aid is different. Your chances of getting more aid are better if you have especially high grades or if you're entering a field of study where the college needs more students. Some colleges make parents write formal appeal letters requesting more aid. Other colleges may suggest private sources of grants

and scholarships that they feel the student would be eligible for. And there may be some colleges that just won't budge. In this day and age, though, bargaining is more and more common. In any case, it never hurts to try!

Merit-Based Scholarships

Most scholarships and grants are given based on financial need. But aid based on merit can also be very rewarding for you. Merit scholarships are harder to get, because there are fewer of them—and also, they are very competitive. But students with good grades, high test scores, and other forms of excellence should give them a try. Plus, even if a student is already eligible for need-based grants, aid based on merit can still add to financial benefits.

Many colleges offer their own merit-based scholarships in athletics or the arts. This is especially true for colleges that are strong in those areas, or whose reputation is based on attracting highly qualified students. Check with your college to see what scholarships are available, and check early to have the best chance of success.

Merit scholarships are given by a wide variety of organizations. Many of them may be located in your community and may not be listed in scholarship books. If so, your chances of getting this kind of aid are even better. Don't forget to check out scholarships given by your own employer, the local Rotary Club, American Legion, the local newspaper, your church or temple, and other civic organizations.

Counselors Can Help You

It's often a great advantage to actually meet and talk with counselors who know the financial aid world well. They can help locate sources of aid and steer you away from sources that may be a waste of your time.

These counselors can be found both at the high school and college level. Get to know them, bribe them, bother them, cajole them, whatever it takes! Their job is to help you, and they are on your side. As they say, "It's who you know."

Plus, if your parents meet with one of these counselors and tell them that their son or daughter must go to college, and that the grants and scholarships to pay for it must be found, these counselors will more often than not appreciate your ambition. Then they will find a way to make it happen!

To Sum Up

As we have discussed in this chapter, the best way to get started in your quest for financial aid is to send away for your FAFSA packet. Once that has been completed, parents and students will know whether they are eligible for federal need-based aid. If you're not eligible, or if you are seeking even more financial aid, you may then wish to pursue sources of merit-based aid as described in this chapter.

Talk to your high school and college counselors and take advantage of their expertise. Check the bookstores and online search services for sources of information on scholarships and grants. And above all, use the listings in Free Cash Grants Vol. 2 to get you started on your quest for scholarships, grants, and loans from Federal, State, and private sources!

Chapter 2
Planning for Parents

These days, wise parents begin planning for their child's college education as soon as they are born. This planning continues through the child's life in the form of money put into accounts that will yield high interest and high gains.

But even if you have never put away a cent, your child can still go to college. The financial need can be met with grants, scholarships and loans. Plus, you can always research low-cost schools if money is particularly tight. Just remember, when there's a will, there's a way. As they say in college, it pays to do your homework!

But most importantly, don't grab the reins from your graduate-to-be. Help your kids choose the college, but don't make the final decision for them. Offer to take them on visits to schools, but in the end, let them decide which ones they like best. If your son or daughter feels they've been railroaded, all the time (and money) you spend on their college education may be wasted.

Savings Tips

Contrary to popular belief, parents are not penalized for saving money for a child's college education. When the financial aid forms are evaluated by federal analysts, only six percent of the parent's assets are entered into the equation. That means that if they have saved $40,000, only $2,400 will be counted as part of the parent's total contribution.

Parents are advised to keep these college funds in their own name, though. When students have assets in their names, 35 percent is counted. Parents can avoid this situation by switching any accounts in the child's name to the parent's name at least one year before applying for financial aid.

Investment Tips

<u>Financial experts say that parents should be prepared to pick up at least a third of the total college costs.</u> With an average college education costing $50,000, that is about $17,000 over four years. This is not a small sum, and most parents are aware of this fact.

However, studies have shown that parents could do better investing their kid's college savings money. About half of parents put the money in certificates of deposit, savings accounts, or money market mutual funds. These investments don't produce a big enough return to put you over the top.

<u>Financial experts advise parents to invest in stock mutual funds for the best return on their investment.</u> These funds offer rates of return that will keep up with both inflation and rising tuition fees. What's more, many will waive initial investment minimums if the parent make automatic deposits every month. These deposits can be as little as $50 or $100 per month.

Analysts also say to avoid investments like as annuities or cash value life insurance. Although both can defer paying taxes on the investment, they also have costly withdrawal penalties if you need the money before you planned.

A Word on the Stock Market

The younger your child is when you begin to invest in his college education, the more aggressive you can be in your investment portfolio. If a parent begins investing before the child is a teenager, there is time to ride out short-term stock market fluctuations. Chances can be taken, because there is time to recover from market dips.

<u>Some well-respected analysts, including *Money* magazine's Marguerite Smith, say that after the student reaches age 14, parents should sell their stocks and buy into fixed income and cash investments.</u> This creates a "safe haven" for the money. The risks have been taken already, and hopefully, the college savings fund has increased handsomely because of it. Now, it's time to make sure that the capital is preserved. Smith recommends Treasury Bonds, Series EE U.S. Savings Bonds, and CDs.

If parents are nervous about risks of the stock market, they can invest up to 25 percent in fixed-income investments such as bonds and bond mutual funds.

Insider's Tip:

Home Equity loans are often an attractive choice for parents looking for alternative ways to finance their child's education. Many, though, have a hard time deciding whether to take a lump sum or establish a home equity line of credit. We suggest that you establish a line of credit, because it will keep you from having to reapply for money if necessary, and also cost you much less in interest payments.

Prepaid Tuition Plans

Almost half of the states in the union now offer plans for parents to prepay their child's tuition by investing over the years. Parents make a contract with the state that says that they can pay for four years' tuition at current rates at a state college. For this reason the Prepaid plan is also sometimes known as a guaranteed tuition plan. When the student does go to college, the tuition will already be paid for, at the rate that was being charged the year the parents entered their contract.

There are some drawbacks, though. You never know where you child will want to go to college, or even if they will want to go to college. If your child decides not to attend a state school, you can get a full refund of the money you invested. However, you cannot get the interest you would have received if you had invested the tuition money.

In other words, before you commit to a prepaid tuition plan, make sure it is what you'll really want—and more importantly, try to make sure it's what your future graduate will really want, too.

Installment and Deferred Tuition Plans

Many schools now offer students the choice to pay for their tuition by making monthly payments. The terms and interest rates depend on the individual school. Some schools will allow a student to defer payment of tuition, sometimes as late as after graduation.

In addition to programs through the schools, there are also private finance companies that will pay your tuition and then collect monthly payments. This arrangement is offered by Academic Management Services. It also allows you to pay tuition costs over a period of 10 months. For more information, call 1-800-635-0120.

Insider's Tip:

Consumer debt is not considered by the Federal government when figuring a parent's ability to pay for their child's education. Parents should not max out their credit cards in the hopes that it will make them look poorer and more in need of Federal financial aid. It doesn't work that way!

Other Loan Sources

See Chapter 5 for information on Federal grants and loans. Like we've said before, every effort is made to help parents come up with the money for their child's education. The following are some additional sources of loans and emergency money.

- The College Board. Parents may apply for an Extra Credit Loan to cover financial costs for as many as four years. These loans don't need to be paid off for 15 years. The College Board also offers Extra Time Loans, which offer loans for only one year at a time. Payment of the loan can be put off until after the student graduates, and repayment can take up to 10 years. For more information call 1-800-874-9390.

- The New England Loan Marketing Association (Nellie Mae) . Parents may receive EXCEL or Share Loans through Nellie Mae. These loans are for between $2,000 and $20,000. Parents have up to 20 years to pay off the loan. For more information call 1-800-634-9308.

- Other lenders with loan programs for parents of college students include Key Education Resources and the Knight College Resource Group, 1-800-225-6783; The Education Resources Institute (TERI), 1-800-255-8374; and ConSern Loans for Education, 1-800-767-5626.

- Academic Management Services. For parents who are totally strapped, this service allows you to pay tuition costs for each college year over a period of 10 months. For more information call 1-800-635-0120.

- The College Resource Center. Parents may borrow up to $50,000. The interest rate is the prime rate plus 2.5 percent, plus an application fee of three percent. For more information call 1-800-477-4977.

Financial Aid

In Chapter 1, we discussed applying for need-based financial aid through the FAFSA program. Here are some issues about filling out those forms that are specific to parents.

Divorce

If you and your spouse have divorced, then the parent who has taken care of the student for the longest period of time in the last year should be

the one to fill out the FAFSA. Sometimes, a college will ask for information about the other parent, but it is not a requirement. If the parent who takes care of the student is remarried, then the finances of the stepparent will be taken into consideration. In that case, the other natural parent will play no role at all. Other special family circumstances can be discussed with a financial aid officer at the college.

Job Loss

What happens if a parent has lost his or her job since the previous year's tax returns have been filed? In that case, the family income could be significantly lower than what is shown on tax returns. In these cases, projected income for the coming year can be used instead. Parents will need to speak with financial aid officers directly and provide documentation about their financial picture.

Insider's Tip:

A small but growing number of colleges are participating in a pilot program known as GATE (Guaranteed Access to Education). This federal student loan defers interest until after the student graduates. It offers a 13-year repayment plan, and rates are lower if the loans are paid off within the first five years. The terms of these attractive loans are "bettered" only by subsidized Stafford Loans. (See Chapter 5 for details on Stafford loans.)

Middle Income Families

Many middle income families feel that they get left behind in the college aid picture, and to some extent, they are right. A family that makes $60,000 may not be able to qualify for much financial aid at a public school. And that family is certainly in a worse position to pay for it than a wealthier family. You'll still get aid, just not as much, and the proportion of the kid's college costs left for you to pay will be higher than for a family with a smaller income.

What's more, most of your aid may consist of loans, which must be paid back after college. Often, students in the middle income range will rack up loans of tens of thousands of dollars, and this credit weight can be a burden. The student's career and lifestyle choices after school can even be limited because they are forced to make so much money to pay off their loans.

The answer? Be creative. <u>Your middle income status can actually be turned into an advantage.</u> It could be better in the end if you sent your kid to a more expensive private school. If tuition is $20,000 a year instead of $10,000, you can show a greater hardship and as a result, you could be eligible for more financial aid. If you work it right, you could send your student to Stanford for the same money that it might have cost to send him or her to a public university!

Outside Scholarships

Parents may be concerned that if the student gets scholarships from high school or community sources, their eligibility for financial aid from the college will decrease. But the formula actually considers these grants and scholarships as part of the family's contribution—so you are not penalized.

The Money is Out There!

The message of this chapter reads loud and clear: <u>there's no reason for parents to hold back on sending their kids to college.</u> If a college meets your student's educational, social, and personal needs, try not to let finances get in the way. The higher degree of hardship that tuition and other costs present, the more financial aid you are entitled to. Granted, finding it may take a bit of work, but it will be worth it in the end.

The fact that you are taking an active role in your child's college education sends a good message. Your child will see that it matters to you that they get a good education. He or she will see that it matters so much, you are willing to put the effort into making it work.

This alone will make them more likely to value their education, and it will make them more likely to succeed once they get to college. Too many kids enter college with an indifferent attitude, partly because the college they are attending means nothing to them. That is money poorly spent. It may have been cheaper to send them there, but in the end, it was a total waste. If you are going to spend the money for college, make sure it's going to be worthwhile experience.

It Helps to Aim High!

The quality of college that a student attends often sets a quality standard for the rest of their lives. The caliber of students at better schools is higher. The quality of teachers is higher. So, we advise you to look at colleges that fits your student's needs the best . . . that will give them the best start on their adult lives. Then work backwards to create a financial plan that will make it happen.

For example, Harvard costs nearly $28,000 a year in tuition alone. But if your child's brain is hungry enough for a challenge like Harvard, then that's what it should get. Call Harvard's financial aid office. Grill them. Make it happen. Don't take the opposite approach, which is to figure what you can afford and then offer that to your child.

The nation's education system was designed to make it possible for any child to get the education they are entitled to. Using the methods outlined in this book, you can make the system live up to its potential!

Chapter 3
Planning for Students

Reams have been written about choosing the right college. The usual advice goes something like this: Don't just go on prestige. Find a campus that feels comfortable to you. Visit at least six schools and get a feel for the students and the professors.

The experts say to ask questions like these: Does the school feel like your style? Is it strong in your area of interest? What is the ratio of students to teachers? Is the library strong, and suited to your major? How many freshman stay all four years? How many students graduate in just four years? These are all important questions.

But we also suggest a good bout of soul searching. This is your college education. It's not for your parents or your friends, and it's not for your future employers. It costs a lot of money to go to school. Make sure the school you pick is the right one for you.

Don't Let Money Stand in Your Way!

Also, DO NOT let the cost of a school influence your decision. If it seems expensive, THAT'S OKAY. Using the techniques in this book, you'll find the money. If the cost seems completely out of the question, just take a deep breath. It still shouldn't affect your decision. It just means that you'll have to be that much more creative in finding money.

It might mean taking a part time job to help out. But we've said it before and we'll say it again: pick the school that feels right to you. Pick the school that feels like it will challenge you and fulfill you and help you to become the person you know is waiting to emerge. And after you've picked the right school, then figure out how to pay for it.

This can be tricky, because your parents are the ones who will most likely foot a good portion of the bill. It may seem selfish for you to ask them to finance an expensive education. But as we noted in the previous chapter,

it often costs your parents the same amount to send you to a low-priced school as to a high-priced school. In some cases, they'll pay EVEN LESS to send you to a high-priced school, because you'll qualify for more financial aid!

Remember, the financial aid opportunities are greater when the hardship on the family is greater. Take advantage of that fact. We're not encouraging you to attend a high-priced college just for the thrill of it. All we're saying is that you shouldn't let cost be the final decision-making factor. There is simply too much financial aid out there for you to think that way!

First Things First

You can help yourself pay for college as soon as you begin high school—and we don't mean by getting a job. We mean by getting good grades! Good grades will save you and your parents lots of money. Good grades will help you qualify for more financial aid. You might even get enough aid so you won't need a part-time job while you're in college.

The students with the best grades get the best merit scholarships—it's as simple as that. The better your grades, the more scholarships and grants you will be eligible for. And with the expense of college, you'll want to have all the help you can get.

Also, if you have great grades, colleges make you better financial aid offers. Colleges want bright students because it helps them build their reputation as a good school. They want to encourage a highly academic atmosphere on campus, and they can do so only if they have students who are serious about their studies.

Good Grades = Good Bargaining!

When it comes time to negotiate with a school about the amount of financial aid you'll receive, you are in a great bargaining position if you have good grades. Bargaining for financial aid is more common than you might think. Students with high grade point averages may be accepted at six or seven schools, and then they play one against the other to get the best financial aid deal. <u>Some schools will give exceptionally bright kids a free ride, free tuition and breaks on housing costs, just to get that student at their school.</u> This is especially if the student is entering an obscure course of study that is not already filled with capable students.

The SAT and ACT

You also want to get good test scores on the SAT or ACT. Success on these tests isn't so much about being smart as about knowing how to take the test. Many books have been written about how to do well on these tests. Before you take the tests, get the books. Put time into studying them. Do the things they tell you to do. Bone up on your algebra, review your American history, and get a good night's sleep before you go in there. Again, you will be doing yourself a big favor. You'll thank yourself when a $3,000 grant check arrives in your mailbox!

When you are in high school, it's hard to see how important these scores will be for you later on. Like good grades, they will help you get into the college you want, and once you are there, they will help you pay for it. Your parents will be much more willing to help you pay for college if you have already done the two best things that you can do to help them—which are to get the best grades and test scores that you possibly can.

Extracurricular Activities

Although test scores and grades are the most important, colleges also look at your extracurricular activities. Don't just think in terms of sports, class officer positions, and volunteer groups. Show that you have personality. Show them that you are unique. This can be through travel, or through an interesting job such as fundraising for the local symphony, taking in stray animals at the pound, working on a political campaign, or developing a recycling program.

Dealing with Problem Parents

We've already explained that if you get good grades and test scores, it's easier to convince your parents that they should help you out with college. But there can be problems.

For instance, some parents will flat out refuse to help. They will say that they would rather not fill out financial aid forms. They may think that if they refuse to help, it will prove that you are on your own and are in desperate need of financial help. But that is the wrong idea. The system doesn't work that way.

<u>Your parents must fill out the FAFSA forms for you to qualify for financial aid.</u> There is no way of getting around it. Tell them that it does not obligate them for anything, but that you will NOT be eligible for any aid unless they fill out the forms. If they fill out the forms, then even if they refuse to pay any money, at least you are free to get loans, grants and scholarships on your own.

Some parents may also think that they make too much money to qualify for financial aid. Again, convince them to fill out the forms anyway. They may be pleasantly surprised!

If your parents have divorced, then the parent who takes care of you should fill out the forms. If that parent is remarried, then that stepparent's income counts on the form as well. If your parents are in the midst of a divorce, ask the parent that will most likely be taking care of you in the future to fill out the forms.

> ### Insider's Tip
>
> Some students think that if they apply for financial aid, they will look less attractive to prospective colleges, and it might make them not get accepted. This is not the case. Almost all schools have a policy of deciding whether a student should be accepted without even being aware of whether they have applied for student aid. So go for it! Apply for aid!

You Are Not Alone

If your parents are refusing to pay for college, or being hesitant about filling out forms, don't feel alone. Many students completely miss going to college because they have parents who don't understand the value of an education. Or the parents may feel threatened by the fact that the student wants to move away to attend college. This is especially true of parents who themselves did not attend college. They may not want you to break away from them. They may think that you don't need college, or that if you want to go, you should pay for it yourself.

Don't let their point of view become a hindrance to you. <u>Tell them that you cannot be declared legally "independent" until you are 24 years old.</u> Until then, you need them to cooperate. If you want to go college, just keep working on them. If it seems hopeless, talk to your high school counselor, and ask if he or she will help.

If you are not 24 years old, the only other way that you can be considered "independent" is if you are married, you are in the Armed Forces, are an orphan or ward of the court, or you have one or more children.

If your parents are not interested in helping you with your pursuit of financial aid, then read Chapter 5. It explains all of the federal grants and scholarships. Once you have gotten your parents to fill out the FAFSA forms, you can do the rest on your own. It'll be a lot tougher, and again, you will need help from financial aid counselors. <u>But you can do it.</u>

Timeline

The remainder of this chapter is broken down into a timeline that will help you get ready for college and find the money to pay for it.

Sophomore Year of High School

You should already be thinking about which colleges you want to attend in your sophomore year. We know this sounds early, but studies have shown that many students regret not getting a start on their searches early. The earlier you start looking at schools, the better prepared you will be. And you find that the more schools you actually visit, and the more counselors you speak with, the more educated and confident you will be about the whole admissions and financial aid process.

When you're visiting colleges, talk to the students there. Ask them if they're happy. Ask them what the school's reputation is like. Ask them if there are other colleges they would have preferred to attend. Feel out the social environment of the college, and even sit in on a class.

Your sophomore year is also a good time to ask yourself about what major course of study would be right. You don't have to decide now—just start thinking about it. If you get an idea of what you'll want to major in, start to tailor your classes and extracurricular activities to prepare yourself for that goal.

In October, you should also take the Preliminary SAT test. It will help get you prepared for the real SAT. For a schedule of test times, talk to your high school counselor or call the PSAT Educational Testing Service at (609) 771-7070.

And don't forget, get good grades!

Insider's Tip

Experts in the counseling field are often asked to help students decide how to choose a major. Increasingly, they tell students to ask the following questions: "What do other people think is special about me? What talents do I have that can best serve society?" This takes the question away from "What do I think I'm good at," and can bring a helpful perspective.

Junior Year of High School

Continue your research on colleges of your choice. If you are online, you can find directories of college's home pages at:

http://akebonon.standfor.eduyahoo/education

and

http://www.edu8001.people/cdmello

Talk with your parents more about college. Ask them if they will drive you to some schools. Ask them if they have thoughts about how they might help you pay for college. Begin to look through scholarship directories online, or in your high school library. Look through the scholarship listings in Free *Cash Grants Vol. 2.* Let your high school counselor know that you plan to attend college and ask for advice and help in getting ready.

In October, take the PSAT once again. At this time you should also take the National Merit Scholarship Qualifying Test. This test will qualify you for the National Merit Scholarship.

In February, sign up to take either the SAT or the ACT. Or you may want to take both. Colleges only take your highest score. Begin studying for the tests. Many good books are available in general bookstores that will help you prepare.

Start to send away for college admission applications. Take a look at them. Get prepared for the types of questions that they ask. Seeing these forms will help you get a picture in your mind of what you are in for, so you can be prepared in advance. Pay special attention to the essay questions.

In June, if you think they can be of advantage to you, take the Advanced Placement Tests. About 20,000 students take them each year as a way to get into college with advanced status.

Start to compile letters of recommendation. These letters are from employers, teachers and other influential adults who know you. They will be sent along with your college admissions application. They help make you look good.

And don't forget, get good grades!

Insider's Tip

Often the best place to get a good feel for campus life is the dining hall. Most dining halls offer meals to visitors, especially prospective students. Have a meal in the hall and check out the food! It's also a good place to meet new students and talk to them about how they like dorm life and the school.

Senior Year of High School

As soon as your senior year of high school begins, send away for application forms from all of the colleges you are interested in attending. Also request financial aid forms from each college.

Begin to research scholarships. <u>A majority of scholarships and grants have March deadlines, so you want to get started on these early.</u> The more research you do, the better! Talk to your high school counselor for recommendations. And when you visit colleges, ask to talk to the financial aid officers there, too. They can give you real world advice!

Put together your resumé. List jobs that you've held, organizations that you belong to, and awards you've won.

Get copies of FAFSA forms and any other financial aid forms you believe are appropriate. You can get these forms from your high school counselor, or by calling (800) 4-FED-AID. FAFSA is also online at http://www.fafsa.ed.gov. <u>You can send these forms in anytime after January 1. But they must include your parents' tax returns, which aren't due until April 15.</u> So encourage your parents to fill out their taxes early so you can send in your FAFSA as early as possible, preferably in February. Some colleges may requires that you fill out PROFILE forms. This is another type of financial aid. If necessary, fill out these forms, too.

Most colleges require you to apply by December or January. Take your time filling out your application form. Include your resume and transcripts. Write good essays. For help, see Chapter 4 in this book. Try to get all of your applications in the mail by January 1.

After January 1, if you are not happy with your ACT or SAT test scores from your junior year, take one or both of the tests again.

Six weeks after you have sent in your FAFSA or PROFILE forms, you will receive your Student Aid Report (SAR). Read this form carefully. It contains information about how much aid you can expect to receive. If the number seems low, or if mistakes were made, write an appeal. Once you are happy with your SAR, send a copy of Part I to the financial aid office of each college to which you've applied. The final deadline is Aug. 19.

If you haven't received your SAR within six weeks of submitting your financial aid forms, phone the Federal Processor at (319) 337-5665.

In April you will receive notification from the colleges you applied to about whether you have been accepted. Compare the financial aid packages that each college offers you. If you want to, negotiate with the financial aid offices of the colleges to which you've been accepted. Force them to make you a better offer. Then, decide on which college you want. <u>You need to make a decision on which college you want to attend by May 1.</u> When you do, send off your final transcript and loan applications to your chosen college. And pat yourself on the back for a job well done!

Chapter 4
Sailing Through The Application Process

Getting accepted into the college of your choice, like successfully steering a boat, depends on paying attention to the details. And while much of the process follows a standard procedure—the SAT and ACT tests, the application forms, the required personal essays— your success really depends on how much of yourself you can bring to the process. When you bring out your own uniqueness in all that paperwork, your application will get noticed among the hundreds or even thousands of other applicants. This chapter will show you how!

Specifically, we will cover the following areas:

- The SAT and ACT Tests—how to take them for the best results.

- The Application—how to maximize your chances of success.

- The Personal Essay—how to put your best foot forward.

Testing The Waters

You've probably heard a great deal about the SAT (Scholastic Assessment Test) and the ACT (American College Test), and whatever you've heard is probably at least partially true. But don't let the rumors get you down. Yes, the SAT and ACT are tests. Yes, they are timed. So what's a student to do?

First of all, relax. These tests are designed to test your understanding and application of the knowledge you already have. They test your learning in several subject areas using a standardized format. That means the structure of the test is the same each and every time; the only difference is the questions that are asked.

If you have studied the materials sent out by the testing service, and (even better) if you've taken one or more complete sample tests, you'll realize that the only thing you won't be familiar with are the particular questions on the test you are taking.

Why Do I Have To Take These Tests?

Colleges and universities use your scores from the SAT or ACT tests, along with your application, transcripts, letters of recommendation and personal essays, to determine how well you will do when faced with their college studies. The tests are part of an entire package that gives the admissions committee a "feel" for you and your abilities.

But I Don't Do Well On Tests!

You will not be judged primarily on your test scores because most admissions officers realize there could be any number of reasons why your score might not be as high as your other records indicate. Perhaps you had a fight with your boyfriend or girlfriend before taking the test; or you could be one of those people who simply freezes up when faced with exam pressures.

To give your best shot at the test, there are a number of things you can do ahead of time to get a head start. Read on for details!

Hints for Getting the Best Score

One of the best ways of getting used to the tests is to take them before you actually have to. How? <u>Plan to take the PSAT (Preliminary Scholastic Assessment Test), which is given to high school juniors.</u> This can provide invaluable experience for the future. Plus, if your score is high enough, you will qualify for consideration for the National Merit Scholarship Corporation award programs.

If you missed the PSAT, you can prepare yourself by ordering practice tests and taking them. Or, visit your local bookstore and invest in a book or two about how to take these tests. It will be money well spent!

Choosing Which Test to Take

What's the difference between the SAT and the ACT? There used to be an imaginary geographical line—students in the Midwest took the ACT and everyone else took the SAT. Now, however, you can usually take either or both and most colleges will accept either one—but do check with the college(s) you are interested in to see which they prefer.

These tests ARE different from each other. Because they test and measure different skills, they can provide you with a chance to highlight your strengths and downplay your weaknesses.

The ACT includes a science reasoning test and trigonometry questions in the math section; it de-emphasizes vocabulary but tests English grammar; and there is no guessing penalty.

The SAT (officially called the SAT I) does not have a science test, and it does not use trigonometry in its math section. Vocabulary is a strong feature, but English grammar testing is non-existent; and guessing wrong does have penalties.

Depending on the college(s) you choose, you may also be required to take the SAT II's. These are specialized SAT tests, usually given on the same day in the afternoon, that test your knowledge in specific subjects. The test format and testing situation will be the same as the SAT, but the content will focus exclusively on one particular subject.

Registration

When you register for any of these tests, you will be sent free booklets which you definitely should read. These will tell you all about the test and offer clear, easy-to-read suggestions and instructions as well as sample questions, their answers, and detailed explanations about the reasons for those answers.

Because the tests are standardized, you can go into them with enormous advantages if you have learned the "rules" that govern them. For example, the SAT is a three-hour, multiple-choice exam, with six sections that are scored. An experimental section that is not scored is also included. (Note: It's important not to assume you "know" which section is experimental; you don't and slacking off could hurt your score.)

You can order actual tests from the testing service, sign up with a private test preparation school, or seek out test preparation books at your local bookstore or library. The sample tests may be as new as last year and they will contain not only the questions and answers but explanations, showing exactly why each of the choices to the question was right or wrong. The detailed explanations show you how the tests are standardized. Understanding the reason for the correct answer will allow you to approach any other question in that section with the same knowledge when you take the actual test.

Practice Sessions

When you sit down to practice, try to set up your work area as if it were the actual day of the tests. Do the following:

- Be prepared to start your practice exam at 9:00 a.m. sharp. Have several No. 2 pencils sharpened and ready.

- Get up as early as need be to shower, dress, and have breakfast.

- Let everyone know that you are not to be disturbed; shut off the phone, if necessary.

- Have an accurate timer (or a friend who will act as the official timer) to start and stop you.

- Don't take any breaks other than the 10 minutes allowed midway during the official test.

Follow test instructions exactly, starting and stopping as you will be required to do on the test day.

Tips For Test-Taking

- **Memorize The Test Directions** — The instructions for the SAT, ACT, ACT II, and PSAT are always the same. Read them over and over until you learn them by heart. Then you won't have to waste any time on exam day.

- **Do Not "Predict" The Answer Before You Know The Question** — While there is only one correct answer, the creators of the test do not make it easy. At least two and possibly four of the answers may appear correct, especially if you have not thoroughly read the question. Leapfrogging ahead by filling in (in your head) the question before you actually read all of it means that you may think you "see" the answer before you know what the question really is.

- **Remember, You Have The Right To Choose The Question Order** — Although the creators of the test usually put the easier questions first, this does not mean you have to answer each question in order. Because you only have a specified period of time for each section, you must pace yourself. <u>Answer those questions that you can answer quickly first, and mark those that you will come back to if you have the time.</u> On your second trip through, do the same thing, taking the questions that require less effort and marking those you'll come back to later.

- **Fill in the right answers in the right circles** — The answer sheets for these tests are filled with little ovals, and it's easy to mark the wrong oval in an answer or make a mistake in a line number so that all your answers are one line off. Use a blank sheet of paper to keep your marks on the correct line number and always do a quick comparison check of the question and answer numbers.

- **"Guesswork" Need Not Be All Guesswork** — Although the SAT instructions state that there are penalties for guessing, what that mean is that if you guess wrong you will be assessed a penalty. While this is not to be underestimated, you may be able to eliminate some of the obvious incorrect answers and boost your "guess" into a "educated guess."

- **Remember It's All About Pacing** — Thirty minutes is thirty minutes. Depending on the number of questions, you will need to answer one question approximately every 60 seconds. Do not spend too much time on any one question.

- **Quickies Can Add Up** — If you can see that you are running out of time with questions yet unanswered, see if you can find anything that offers a quick turnaround time. For example, a passage that is too long to read may ask you the meaning of a particular word (something that does not require a read-through). But don't panic and just start filling in spaces—you're unlikely to increase your score that way!

• **Final Word** — Remember, these tests are not the "make-it or break-it" factor in admissions officers' decisions. Just do the best you can. Know the rules, understand the reasons behind the answers, and work with practice tests. Review your mistakes and concentrate on your weak areas. Then relax and go for it!

Filling Out The Application

The application form for each college will give you a chance to focus on areas other than test scores. Most college admissions officers view a student's academic record as more important than the SAT and ACT. For one thing, it spans a greater period of time. A student's progress not only in learning but in commitment can be seen from a high school transcript. Do you like challenges? If you do, it will probably show in the type of classes you took and the work you produced in them.

What extracurricular activities and clubs were you involved in? Did you take any leadership roles? Be selective and know what you are capable of. While some people can handle many commitments and rack up honors and awards, others need more time for family or school or themselves. Just choose activities you like and give them your best.

Be Prepared!

Every college's admissions office has preferences about what it wants and doesn't want included with the application. Some want the form alone; others are happy to see additional information included; and still others accept only official attachments, such as letters of recommendation, and nothing else.

You can save yourself some rushing around later by preparing those items you would like to include, or know will be required, while waiting for your applications to arrive. If your list of extracurricular and community activities is extensive, consider making up a resume. If you have a list of awards and honors, include them on the resume, too.

Letters of Recommendation

Select the people from whom you want letters of recommendation. Don't just limit your choices to teachers or advisors. There are many other

people who can provide an additional perspective. These could include people you worked with in a job or volunteer position, a member of your church's clergy, an athletic coach, or any other person who has known you for a long time.

Letters of recommendation give the admissions committee another look at you in addition to the application and your personal essay. Therefore, choose people who are familiar with your academic progress, your other skills, and your growth as a person. Do not tell them what to say. Just make sure the persons recommending you understand what topics they need to cover. Choose people who can write well and give a clear picture of your accomplishments.

Tell your references why you have chosen them and ask if they will do it. It takes time and effort on their part to write a good recommendation, so give them at least one month prior to the deadline. Give them a copy of your transcript and a list of your accomplishments and activities; this will help them write their letter.

Don't forget to include a stamped, self addressed envelope so all they need to do is drop it in the mailbox. And be sure to thank them for their efforts and let them know which school you finally decide to attend!

Doing the Paperwork Right the First Time

College applications are nothing more than a pile of information separated into little boxes on a form. These forms are usually the college's first contact with you, and it's where you make your first impression. The form's appearance, plus spelling, grammar, punctuation and readability do count.

It's a good idea to photocopy each application form several times before you begin to fill it out. Then it won't matter if you make mistakes—you can just transfer your final copy to a clean form once you get it all down right.

Most important of all, don't forget to include the application fee!

- **Read all the instructions carefully before you begin** — and follow them exactly. Do not make exceptions to the college's rules and preferences. Remember, admissions officers are extremely busy and you don't want to annoy them.

- **Type the information** —unless they specifically request that you use ink. If so, use black ink and print neatly.

Fill in all the spaces, even if the question does not apply to you — That way the admissions office knows you didn't just miss the question. If the question does not apply to you, just print or type N/A, which means that the information is "not applicable." If you list your community and extracurricular activities, honor and awards on a separate piece of paper, use the phrase "See attached."

- **Keep your own FAQ list** — FAQ stands for "Frequently Asked Questions." These are the questions that appear on every application form. You can save yourself time by keeping a master list of the answers to these questions. They might include: the semester you plan to enroll; your state of legal residence and the date you became a resident; your intended program of study and major; the dates you will take or took the SAT or ACT; your Social Security number; date and place of birth; parents' names and addresses; name and address of high school; and a description of your activities, honors and awards.

- **Be honest with your answers** — You will be judged on the entire package you submit. If you exaggerate or misrepresent yourself and this shows up, the college will reject you. Let your application, SAT or ACT scores, recommendation letters and personal essay show the admissions committee who you really are.

- **Get the application in on time** — Get a large wall calendar and use it! Mark the deadline date for each application and then go backwards from that to today and mark dates that (1) are the earliest you can mail it in; (2) a one-week range that is still early enough to beat out many others; and (3) the deadline. Be sure to keep a copy of all your completed applications in a file folder until you have been officially accepted.

- **Attachments/Recommendations** — Admissions committees are extremely busy, with some of them judging thousands of applications for a single semester. Unless the application encourages you to submit extra items, it is probably better not to include them. Your best bet is to follow their rules exactly. Letters of recommendation are one of the best ways of supplementing your application, and they are usually read with interest. If the college allows it, add a resume or personal "fact sheet."

- **Financial aid applications**—If you will be seeking scholarships, grants, student loans or other forms of financial aid, pay special attention to deadlines. With the exception of federally insured student loans, most monies are limited and the earliest applicants have the best chance. Even government-backed loans have early deadlines, so be sure to put these on your calendar as well, and keep copies of all paperwork on file.

- **Final Word** — The application is more than just a form—it's your introduction to the colleges of your choice. Make sure it shows you at your best!

> ### Insider's Tip:
>
> Find a teacher, friend, or family member who will critique your entire college application — including your personal essay.

Writing Essays That Get Noticed

Personal essays are the best way the admissions committee has of getting to know you personally. The essay is your chance to highlight something unique about yourself. Generally, the topic is broad enough to allow for creativity and freedom when you write.

Most colleges and universities now require personal essays. Unlike the application and letters of recommendation, the personal essay provides admissions officers with a view of you as a person, allowing them to understand who you are. That's why you alone must write the essay, using words that express your own personality.

What They Want

Simply put, admissions officers are looking for the person behind the application. They want to hear your voice, share your feelings, and learn who you are. You will usually be asked to write the essay about a general topic such as an important personal experience, an influential person or book in your life, a social or political issue that is important to you, the reasons for your career choice, or the best advice you ever received.

What Works Best

The essay should always stay focused on the question presented; that is, be sure you answer the question(s) you are asked. If the question revolves around a personal experience that had a profound impact on your life, you should select one that gave you an understanding you didn't have before or that altered your views or your life. The incident need not have been major, but it should have been important to you.

Keep your essay organized, with thoughts that flow in a clear and logical manner.

The essay should tell a story that you have feelings for. Whether it is presented as humor, satire or a deeply felt revelation, it needs to relate its impact on you in your own words. This is the best place to "show, not tell."

Don't crank out your essay at the last minute. In fact, you should consider writing it over a period of weeks. Take your time to think about the question and re-live the experience. Then write it, refine it, and polish it until it is the very best that you can do.

One essay may work for different colleges and universities. Even if you cannot use the same essay because a different question is asked, most essay questions usually fit into a general mold. You may only need to re-write parts of it to suit another school's requirements.

Formatting Your Essay

Use an outline to set down your experience and its influence on you in a clear and logical manner. Depending on the length requirements, you may want to use a format that includes an introduction, the body of the material, and a conclusion. Within that basic outline, you can add subheadings that will expand upon the general idea or personalize it with quotations, poems, statements, or other unique ideas.

But I Can't Write!

<u>Yes, you can!</u> You can write in your own words, using your own voice. Think about how you might tell this story to someone you trusted completely, sharing all your feelings about it. If it helps, try using a tape recorder to tape yourself telling this story in a natural way. Ask yourself: what happened; what did it feel like; what did I do or not do; how did I react to it; would I prefer to have acted differently and if so, why; what changed in my life as a result of that experience; how do I feel about it now; would I be the person I am today if it hadn't happened?

Suggestions For Getting Started

- **Choosing the Subject, Tone and Content** — Admissions officers want to see you through your eyes. How do you see your growth as a person, a member of your community, your school, and your country? They want to know if you recognize a sense of personal responsibility, a commitment to yourself and others, and your potential for adding value to the college or university and your community.

- **Length Requirements** — If the application form lists one or more short essay questions (generally requiring less than 100 words), you will need to be very focused. Do not deviate from the question and stay within the space provided on the form. Do photocopy the application and practice typing out what you have written until it fits, without crowding, into the allotted space.

The Importance of the Essay

Whenever admissions officers are interviewed about their thoughts and ideas on the process of admissions, it is the personal essay that elicits the strongest reaction. Most of them have the same advice:

Let your writing reflect your voice. In other words, it must be you who comes through in the essay.

Answer the question asked. Yes, let them know who you are and why you are writing what you are writing, but do it within the boundaries of the essay question.

Proofread your essay. This does not mean using the spellchecker on your computer. You can use it as a first step in catching typos, but the spellchecker can be easily fooled. Proofreading means going over what you have written, slowly, reading each word aloud, while looking at each letter to catch any possible errors (such as accidentally leaving the "r" off of "your").

Final Word. Colleges and universities are always on the lookout for a good mix of students who will create an exciting educational environment. You can use your personal essay to project your own uniqueness and convince them that you are worthy of being part of that. Just share yourself in your own way, and you'll make a good impression!

Insider's Tip:

Practice writing your essay months ahead of when it is due. Then, write another one a couple of months later. Compare them. See if you haven't improved! Remember, practice makes perfect.

Chapter 5
Federal Financial Aid

The federal government is in the business to lend, pay or give you money outright in order to help cut down or lower your college education expenses. While you can depend on your family and personal savings to some extent, it's definitely worth your while to take advantage of what many successful graduates know:

• The federal government is the single largest source of financial aid for students.

• There is over $30 billion in federal money available each year in the form of grants, low-interest loans, fellowships and scholarships.

This chapter will help you through the often confusing sea of paperwork and forms to help you realize your dreams. Remember, the Federal government works for you!

Qualifying for Financial Aid

In this section we'll debunk two common myths that may have prevented you from making the first steps toward applying for financial aid:

• **Myth No: 1 — You Have To Be Poor**

• **Myth No: 2 — You Have To Be a High School Student**

Debunking Myth No: 1 — While it's true that grant, work-study and some loan programs are reserved for the neediest students, demonstrating financial need is NOT a requirement for applying for financial aid. There are a number of loan programs where all you have to do to qualify is to pass a credit check.

Debunking Myth No 2 — You don't have to be fresh out of high school to qualify for aid. You can be any age at all. All you need is a high school diploma, a GED (General Education Development) certificate, or a passing grade on a high school equivalency test approved by the U.S. Department of Education.

Insider's Tip:

No matter what your financial status — you can go to college. Anyone who uses these Federally Funded Grants and Loans can be sure of success!!

Eligibility Requirements

What follows are the rules set by the federal government on WHO can qualify for federal aid. They are:

- You must be a U.S. citizen or eligible noncitizen.

- You need a valid Social Security Number.

- You must be working, or plan to work, on a course of study at a qualified school that leads to an associate, bachelor's, or graduate degree.

- Correspondence or telecommunications courses don't usually qualify.

- Males between the ages of 18-25 must register with the Selective Service. (Women, and males under 18 and over 25, are exempt.)

- You can't be in default on any existing federal student loan, or have already borrowed the maximum amount through any of these programs.

- You must sign a "Statement of Educational Purpose" where you promise that all money received from federal student aid will be used only for your educational expenses.

- You must maintain passing grades to continue to receive federal aid.

Guidelines for First-Time Applicants

As we discussed in Chapter 1, you'll need to fill out a Free Application for Federal Student Aid (FAFSA). This is available in paper form at your high school guidance counselor or by mail from Federal Student Aid Programs, P.O. Box 84, Washington, DC. You can also call 1-800-4-FED-AID (800-433-3243); the TDD number for the hearing impaired is 1-800-730-8913.

There are three choices for how to fill out your FAFSA:

• Paper Form

• Electronically with FAFSA Express software (free) from the above address, at your school or local library, or call 1-800-801-0576.

• Online by downloading the software through the U.S. Department of Education's Website at http://www.fafsa.ed.gov. This is a user-friendly website with extensive online instructions. If you apply online, remember that your original signature must be submitted (the software prints out a signature page). The Department will hold your application for 14 days while waiting for the signature page.

How to Fill Out Your FAFSA

Review the FAFSA instructions carefully before proceeding and be sure to watch out for questions on income. It will help to have certain important records immediately at hand. Be prepared to make copies of the documents that you need to include with your application.

Required Documents

- Prior year U.S. Federal, state, and local income tax returns from one or both parents

- W2 forms and other records of money

- Statements or records of untaxed income (welfare, social security, veterans' benefits)

- Current bank statements

- Records of stocks, bonds, and other investments

- Driver's license, Social Security Number

- Promissory notes, loan disclosure statements

- Student and parent signatures must be included

Insider's Tip:

Take your time filling out the FAFSA. Remember, incomplete forms will be returned, delaying your loan or eliminating your chances of receiving aid altogether!

When to Apply for Financial Aid

Aid is generally awarded on a first come, first serve basis. File your FAFSA as soon as possible after January 1 of the year you're applying for, and no later than June 30. No exceptions! You can't apply before this date or send information before January 1.

File your taxes as early as possible so you can have your return at hand to send with the FAFSA. Ask your parents ahead of time to complete their return early. Your goal is to send in your FAFSA no later than February.

You must apply or reapply for federal aid every year that you want to be considered. Aid doesn't travel with you when you change schools. Check with your college financial aid office for steps you can take to keep your federal aid.

If you apply by mail, response time should be 4-6 weeks; electronic applications take 1 week. If you don't hear anything after 4 weeks, call 1-319-337-5665 (Monday-Friday, 9am-8pm EST). The federal processor will send you a Student Aid Report (SAR). The SAR will tell you your Expected Family Contribution (EFC), stating how much your family is expected to pay towards your college costs. Review your SAR carefully for any errors; make corrections on Part 2 of the SAR, and return it to the address noted on the report.

Mail or bring Part 1 of your original SAR (don't forget to make copies!) to the colleges you've applied to. The college financial aid offices will verify the information from your FAFSA, determine your aid eligibility, and then send you a financial aid award letter. This letter states the amount of aid you're eligible for and the types of aid (loans, grants, work-study) that make up your total aid package.

Renewal Applicants

In most cases, you can fill out the Renewal Free Application for Federal Student Aid. Check with your college financial aid office. This form has fewer questions to answer, and information on the form is preprinted from the previous year, including corrections.

Insider's Tip:

Rather than going into debt at a four year university, many students opt for community colleges, which can cut overall college costs in half. Often general education classes are better taught at community colleges, since professors are less interested in their own research and more interested in the students.

Types of Federal Financial Aid Programs

This section provides an easy reference guide to the three basic categories of federal financial aid programs and the options available within those categories. Included are program descriptions, eligibility, amount of award given, interest rate, repayment schedule, minimum repayment, interest subsidy, and origination fees (if applicable). Not all of these financial aid programs are available to everyone; read carefully to see which programs you qualify for.

I. Grants

Grants are a form of financial aid that provide funds which do not have to be paid back. There are two types of Federal Grants.

A. Federal Pell Grants:

- General Description: One of two of the largest higher education grant programs. Funding is guaranteed by the U.S. Department of Education. Each participating school receives enough money to pay eligible students.

- How to Apply: Contact your school for application information.

- Eligibility: Undergraduates, or students who have not yet earned a bachelor's or professional degree. Reserved for the neediest students only.

- Amount of Award Given: Varies each year, depending on program funding. For 1997-1998 award year, the maximum award per student was $2,470. Students must usually apply for other grants or loans to supplement their Federal Pell Grant.

B. Federal Supplemental Educational Opportunity Grants (FSEOG)

- General Description: One of the two of the largest higher education grant programs along with Federal Pell Grants (see above). Unlike Federal Pell Grants, FSEOGs are NOT backed by U.S. Department of Education, and do not guarantee that all eligible students will be paid. Schools are allocated a limited amount of funds per award year; when this money is gone, no more awards are given. Apply early for best results!

- How to apply: Contact your school for application procedures.

- Eligibility: Undergraduates, or those students who have not yet earned a bachelor's or professional degree. Candidates must prove extreme financial need. Priority is given to Federal Pell Grant recipients.

- Amount of Award Given: Ranges from $100 to a maximum of $4,000 per year.

II. Work-Study Programs

A. Earn-As-You-Learn Program

- General Description: In the Earn-As-You-Learn Program, students are paid money while in college by working part-time on campus or in community-related services. Jobs pertain to the student's course of study.

- Eligibility: Undergraduate or graduate students. Must demonstrate financial need.

- Amount of award given: Federal Work Study (FWS) awards are administered by FAA's at participating schools; amount varies per award year. Salaries are at least federal minimum wage or higher, depending on type of work and skills required, but the total amount does not exceed the total FWS award.

B. Americorps National and Community Service Plan

- General Description: This national service program allows high school graduates to fund their college education or repay student loans by working before, during or after college. Call 1-800-942-2677 for more information, or visit their web site at www.cns.gov.

III. Education Loans

- General Description: Government sponsored loans for students and/or parents who can borrow money for education either from a lender (bank, credit union, or S&L), the U.S. Department of Education, or directly from the school. Must be paid back, but interest rates are low, from 5 percent to 9 percent. Some loans are subsidized, which means that the student pays no interest while in school or during grace periods. There are two types of Education Loan Programs — Federal Family Education Loan Program (FFELP), and the Federal Direct Student Loan Program (FDSLP).

A. Federal Family Education Loan Program (FFELP)

- General Description: Government-sponsored loans for students and/or parents are available through a financial institution, i.e., banks, credit unions, S&L's, or your school. Most accredited colleges and universities participate in this program. To find a qualified lender, contact your school's FAA or your state's guarantee agency; call 1-800-4-FED-AID (1-800-433-3243) for your agency's address and telephone number. There are several types of FFELP Programs, described below:

1. FFELP PLUS Loans:

- General Description: Provides loans for parents to help finance their children's education.

- How to Apply: Parents must send the school a completed PLUS loan application, available from a lender or from their state's guaranty agency. It will then be sent to a lender for evaluation. No FAFSA is needed.

- Eligibility: Parents of full- or part-time undergraduate students. Parents can finance more than one child's education per year. Proof of financial need unnecessary; (ask your school if you need to fill out a FAFSA), but a credit check is required. Relatives with good credit can also endorse the loan, paying it back if parents cannot do so.

- Amount of Award Given: Maximum loan is the total cost of yearly tuition, minus other aid received.

- Interest Rate: Varies, with a cap at 9 percent.

- Term of Repayment: Up to 10 years

- Minimum Repayment: $600 per year or $50 per month

- Repayment begins: No grace period; begins 60 days after final loan funds (disbursements) are issued by the lender.

- Origination fees: Up to 4%

2. FFELP Stafford Loans

General Description: Provides low-interest loans to students. There are two types of Stafford Loans — subsidized Stafford loans and unsubsidized Stafford loans. Students can receive a subsidized Stafford loan and an unsubsidized Stafford loan for the same enrollment period.

a.) FFELP Subsidized Stafford Loans:

- General Description: A type of education loan where the federal government pays the interest on your loan while you are still in school and for six months after you graduate.

- How to apply:

1.) A Completed FAFSA or Renewal FAFSA form.

2.) A Federal Stafford Loan Application

3.) A promissory note from your school, lender or state guarantee agency.

- Eligibility: Undergraduate and graduate students enrolled in school at least half-time. Proof of financial need is necessary.

- Amount of award given: Undergraduate students can borrow up to $2,625 in their first year of full time study to a maximum of $5,500 after three years of study. Graduate students can borrow up to $8,500.

• Interest rate: Variable, with a cap of 8.25 percent.

• Repayment schedule: Up to 10 years.

• Minimum Repayment: $600 per year or $50 per month

• Repayment begins: After a 6-month grace period after leaving school.

• Origination fees: Up to 4%

b.) Unsubsidized Stafford Loans:

• General Description: A type of low-interest loan for students who do not qualify for subsidized Stafford loans. Students are responsible for paying the interest that builds up on their loan from the first payment until it's paid in full.

• How to Apply: See Subsidized Stafford Loans

• Eligibility: Full- or part-time undergraduate or graduate students. Proof of financial need unnecessary. Amount of award given: Depends on status of student. Undergraduates with access to parental support, or dependent students, can receive up to $2,625 in their first year of study to a maximum of $5,500 in their third year of study. Undergraduates without access to parental support, or independent students, can receive up to $2,625 in their first year of study to a maximum of $10,500 in their third year of study. Graduate students can borrow up to $18,500 each year of study to a maximum of $138,500.

• Interest Rate: Variable, with an 8.25 percent cap.

• Repayment schedule: Up to 10 years.

• Minimum repayment: $600 per year, or $50 per month.

• Repayment begins: 6 months after leaving school

• Origination fees: Up to 4%

B. Federal Direct Student Loan Program (FDSLP)

- General Description: Government-sponsored loans available directly from the U.S. Department of Education. Most accredited colleges and universities participate in this program. There are three types of these loans:

1. Federal Direct PLUS Loans

- General Description: The same as a FFELP Direct loan, except that the lender is the U.S. Department of Education.

- How to Apply: Fill out a Direct PLUS Loan Application and a Promissory Note, available from your school's financial aid office. No FAFSA is necessary.

2. Federal Direct Stafford Loans:

- General Description: The same as a FFELP Stafford loan; the only difference is that the lender is the U.S. Department of Education.

- How to Apply: After your FAFSA or Renewal FAFSA has been processed, read carefully, complete, and sign a promissory note provided by your school.

3. Federal Perkins Loan:

- General Description: A low interest (5 percent) loan for students. Your school acts as the lender using government allocated funds. Loans are repaid directly to your school.

- How to apply: Contact your school for application procedures.

- Eligibility: Full- or part-time undergraduate or graduate students who can prove exceptional financial need. Priority is offered to those who have received Pell Grants (see above).

- Amount of Award: For undergraduates, $3,000 per year to a maximum of $15,000; for graduate students, $5,000 per year to a maximum of $30,000.

- Interest rate: Fixed, at 5%

- Repayment schedule: Up to 10 years.

- Minimum repayment: $480 per year or $40 per month

- Repayment begins: 9 months after leaving school, different for those attending half-time.

Postponement and Cancellation of Loans

Payments on all educational loans discussed in this chapter can be postponed or suspended temporarily (called a deferment) under certain circumstances. In some cases the government will pay your interest during a deferment. You can also be granted forbearance, or a temporary adjustment of your payment schedule, in cases of financial or medical hardship or other reasons.

If you become totally or permanently disabled, or become a full-time nurse, medical technician or serve in the Peace Corps, your financial obligation can be cancelled (discharged) altogether. In any case, you must apply in writing and supply the appropriate documentation to your lender who makes the ultimate judgement on all deferments, forbearances, and cancellations.

Repayment Options

Now that you've had a chance to go over the different types of loans available to you, we've included below the various repayment plans that will make it easier for you to pay back your loans. As a first time borrower, building a credit history, the last thing you want to do is to take on more debt than you can pay back.

You'll be out of school in no time at all, and soon you'll be required to make regular monthly payments, so it helps to plan way ahead. Before you sign anything, ask your lender to run through these repayment plans in detail; this is required by law. Your college financial aid office is also a good source of advice.

Standard Repayment Account

You'll be required to pay a fixed amount each month, at least $50, for up to 10 years. The length of your actual repayment period depends on the amount of your loan. You pay the least amount of interest (the cost you pay to borrow money) using this plan.

Graduated Repayment Account

Using this plan, your interest-only initial monthly payments start out low, and then increase gradually every two years over a period of 12-30 years. Although your monthly payments would be around 40 percent lower than what you'd pay using the Standard Repayment, you'll pay more interest over the life of your loan, because the principal (the total amount you borrow) is not paid down as quickly.

Loan Consolidation

With loan consolidation, you can combine any of the following loans — subsidized Stafford, unsubsidized Stafford, PLUS, and Perkins — into a single loan with a single monthly payment. It offers lower initial monthly payments, sometimes with an extended repayment term; this will increase the total cost of your loan.

Income Sensitive Repayment

When your monthly gross income dips, payments are smaller. Alternatively, when your income increases, you'll pay more.

Prepayment

All federally sponsored loans allow partial or full payment of your entire loan at any time without penalty.

You're On Your Way!

Use the Glossary below to help you navigate the world of Federal grants and loans. The same words apply to other types of grants and loans as well, so keep this glossary handy for a quick review. Next, see Chapters 6 and 7 for even more programs that will be of special interest to you—and don't forget to start looking over the scholarship listings in *Free Cash Grants Vol. 2!*

Glossary of Terms

Default — When you fail to pay your education loan or loans.

Deferment — A period of time when borrowers can have their loan payments suspended temporarily. Must meet certain criteria and be approved by the lender.

Disbursement — Loan funds issued by a lender.

Financial Aid Administrator (FAA) — Official at your College Financial Aid Office who provides important information about federal programs and college programs.

Forbearance — A temporary adjustment to borrower's repayment schedule for reasons of financial or physical hardship.

Grace period — A specific period of time after graduation when loan payments do not need to be made.

Guaranty agency — State agency that insures and guarantees student loans for lenders and administrates FFELP loans for the federal government.

Interest-only payment — Covers interest owed on a loan but excludes the principal balance.

Interest — What it costs you to borrow money.

Lender — Financial institutions, state agencies or educational institutions that loan money to borrowers.

Origination Fee — Fee deducted from the principal, that goes to the federal government to offset the costs of subsidizing borrowers under the FFELP.

Principal — Amount you borrow and on which you pay interest.

Promissory note — Written agreement between borrower and lender that includes all terms and conditions on which you promise to pay your loan.

Subsidized Stafford Loans — A type of education loan where the federal government pays the interest on your loan while you are still in school and for six months after you graduate.

Unsubsidized Stafford Loans — A type of low interest loan for students who don't qualify for subsidized Stafford loans. Students are responsible for paying the interest that builds up on their loan from the first payment until it's paid in full.

Chapter 6
Military Programs

On the average in the United States, the costs of college education are estimated at $26,000 per year for a public college and $53,000 at a private institution. But the military can help defray or totally eliminate these costs. Benefits can be gained by using ROTC scholarships to cut costs of a public university education, by enrolling at a military academy, or by taking advantage of a long list of scholarships available to both enlisted and veteran personnel.

All About the ROTC

ROTC stands for the Reserve Officers Training Corps. The mission of ROTC is to develop future officer leadership of the Armed Forces, and to motivate young people to be better citizens. ROTC is offered by the Army, Navy and Air Force.

By offering low cost or free education, ROTC encourages the recruiting, training, evaluating, selecting and commissioning quality people for military service. Nearly 70 percent of the commissioned officers in the U.S. Army come out of ROTC programs.

In addition, Junior ROTC programs are also offered in more than 475 high schools. Participation in the high school program affords cadets special consideration in military academy appointments, or early promotions once they are in the service.

ROTC, the Scholarship Leader

ROTC is one of America's leading sources of college scholarships. Each year, about 3,600 students receive ROTC scholarships, out of about 25,000 applicants.

ROTC scholarships are not based on financial need. Instead, they are awarded on merit. Merit is exhibited in academic achievement, test scores, and extracurricular activities, such as sports, student government, or part-time work.

ROTC scholarships can be worth more than $50,000. Students who receive full ROTC scholarships are given a virtual free ride through college. The scholarship pays for all tuition, fees, and textbooks through the student's four years of college. Often, in addition, students receive $100 a month spending money! Students are also eligible to receive tax free stipends of up to $1,500 a year, to be spent as they wish.

One, two, and three year scholarships are also available to students already enrolled in college.

Many individual universities offer their own incentives to students who are awarded ROTC scholarships. These can include such benefits as free room and board, or partial payment of rent. They may also include individual scholarships that reward high grade point averages.

The Nuts and Bolts

Students who accept an ROTC scholarship agree to serve five years of active duty after they graduate. A student may back out of this obligation without penalty before their sophomore year. After that, backing out may incur a penalty, such as being forced to serve active duty as a enlisted service member, or being required to pay back the financial aid received.

Students who enroll in ROTC are not joining the Army or other Armed Forces, and they do not have to go to boot camp. Students don't "join" ROTC, they simply enroll in its classes.

The ROTC program is divided into two phases. The Basic Course, which is taken during the first two years of college, teaches Armed Forces history, organization and structure. Techniques and principles of leadership and management are stressed. During this phase, students have absolutely no military obligation.

The advanced course, taken in the last two years of college, concentrates on tactical operations and military instruction, as well as advanced techniques of management, leadership, and command.

While in the advanced course, students have a commitment to serve in the Armed Forces on active duty or in a reserve component. ROTC students are also required to attend advanced camp at no cost during the summer between their junior and senior years. At the five-week the camp, they get a hands-on feeling for the Armed Forces.

The courses are intended to give the ROTC student a variety of leadership and management skills that will help them become a U.S. Army officer, or have a successful civilian career. More than 12,000 military officers come of the ROTC each year.

Other Requirements

During college, ROTC classes usually take a commitment of five hours per week. While in the ROTC training classes, students are required to wear a uniform and otherwise act in a manner befitting a military officer. But the rest of the student's time is spent on his or her other classes and normal student social activities.

The ROTC scholarships are a very tempting offer. They allow students a free ride through college. But students should think long and hard before they accept such a scholarship about whether they will "fit in" to a military-type regimen. This is especially true because of the commitment they make to serve as an officer in the Armed Forces for at least five years after they graduate.

Green to Gold Program

ROTC also helps young enlisted soldiers who have decided to leave active duty in order to attend college. Enlisted soldiers who show officer potential and who have served at least two years on active duty are allowed to voluntarily request discharge from active duty, so that they may enroll in ROTC. They are eligible for full scholarship to earn a bachelor's degree, and they become commissioned upon graduation as a second lieutenant.

For More Information

For more information about ROTC scholarships, contact:

In the Army:
College Army ROTC
PO Box 1688
Ellicott City, Maryland, 21043-9923
1-800-USA-ROTC

In the Navy:
NROTC Scholarships
PO Box 27429 NW
Washington D.C. 20038
1-800-327-NAVY

In the Air Force:
AFROTC
Maxwell Air Force Base
Alabama 36112-6663
334-953-7085

Military Academies

While ROTC pays students to attend a public university in exchange for their military service, military academies take students directly into the fold. These academies offer a full four year education, culminating in a bachelor of science degree.

Students receive their four years of college free, paid for entirely by the federal government, plus a monthly stipend of between $100 and $500 a month. During freshman year, though, most of this money is deducted for the costs of uniforms, books, and laundry. Free benefits include room and board, as well as medical and dental care.

The students at these academies enjoy a high degree of prestige. The academies offer rigorous academic training and also strict discipline. Academic ratings are high, and competition is fierce. Some say that the education at the military academies is on par with the best Ivy League schools.

The Inside Picture

While at the academy, students must observe all facets of military decorum, including uniforms and haircut. They must also understand that almost all of their fellow students will be men. Students must serve in the military for at least five years after graduation.

In order to get into the academies, a student must be nominated by a Congressperson from their home state. They may get this nomination after sending in to the academy for a full application packet. Like all academic institutions, military academies take into account grades, test scores, extracurricular activities and personal references. Students must also pass a physical aptitude exam.

The Army, Navy, Air Force, Coast Guard and Merchant Marines all of have their own academies. The most famous of these is the West Point Academy for future Army officers in New York. Marine Corps officers are trained at the Naval Academy.

For More Information

The following are places to contact for information on admission at each of the academies.

Cadet Admissions Office
United States Air Force Academy
Colorado Springs, Colorado, 80840
719-333-2520

U.S. Coast Guard Academy
New London Connecticut 06320-4195
860-444-8444

U.S. Naval Academy
Annapolis, Maryland 21402-5018
1-800-638-9156

U.S. Military Academy
West Point, New York 10996-1967
914-938-4041

Merchant Marines

The U.S. Merchant Marine Academy is located at Kings Point, New York, on the north shore of Long Island. This academy is similar to the other academies, except that students are trained to be officers who will work in a civilian operation. Merchant Marines become civilian officers, even though the corps falls under U.S. Defense Department guidelines.

Close ties exist between the Merchant Marines and the Naval Reserve. Graduates of Kings Point are commissioned as officers in the Naval Reserves because of the similar mandate of the two groups.

Like the other academies, the full costs of tuition are paid for, but students do not receive a monthly stipend. Upon graduation, students become licensed officers in the Merchant Marines, and are required to serve as employees in the maritime industry of the United States for at least five years. Merchant Marine graduates also have the option of becoming a full-time Navy officer.

The Merchant Marines were the first academy to accept women, and women who become merchant marines often encounter fewer restrictions than they would at other academies.

For more information about the Merchant Marine Academy, contact:

Admissions Office
United States Merchant Marine Academy
Kings Point, New York 11024-1699
(516)-773-5000

Merchant Marine Scholarships

Students may receive scholarships of $3,000 a year to study at one of five state Maritime Academies, with the intention of becoming a merchant marine officer aboard vessels for at least five years. These academies are located in California, Maine, Massachusetts, Michigan, and New York.

Other service options for graduates of these schools are to serve as an employee in the U.S. maritime industry, or as a commissioned officer on active duty in an U.S. Armed Forces or in the National Oceanic and Atmospheric Administration.

Students who accept this scholarship must also remain in a reserve unit of an armed force for eight years.

For more information, contact:

Office of Maritime Labor and Training
Maritime Administration
U.S. Department of Transportation
400 7th St. SW
Washington DC 20590
202-366-5755

National Guard and Selected Reserve

Through the GI Bill , anyone who joins the National Guard or Selected Reserve can receive funding to pursue an undergraduate degree or a non-degree program at vocational and technical schools. Even correspondence courses are okay! Typical reservists are eligible for 36 monthly payments while in school. But if they are eligible for educational assistance under other Veterans Administration programs, the payments may extend to 48 months.

For more information, contact:

Assistant Secretary of Defense
Reserve Affairs
Pentagon
Room 2E520
Washington DC 20301-1500
703-697-6631

Vocational Rehabilitation for Disabled Veterans

This program helps veterans who were disabled during service to get the kind of education they need to be independent, and also be employable. Veterans who are accepted into the program have all their tuition, books, fees, supplies, and other college or vocational training services paid for. In addition, they receive a monthly allowance from $333 for a single veteran to $486 for a veteran with two dependents, plus $35 for each dependent more than two.

The program honors a variety of educational opportunities. These include trade, business, or technical schools, college, apprenticeship programs, cooperative farming, and special rehabilitation facilities. Home education is honored when necessary.

For more information, contact:
Department of Veterans Affairs
Central Office
Washington DC 20420
1-800-827-1000 (Connects you with nearest VA regional office.)

Survivors and Dependents Educational Assistance

The Department of Veterans' Affairs provides money to pay for the education of spouses and children of deceased or disabled veterans. This also counts for spouses and children of service personnel who have been listed as Missing in Action or Prisoners of War.

Funds will pay for tuition, books and other fees for college or training courses. In addition, the program provides $404 each month for living expenses to full time students. Three quarter time students receive $304, and half time students receive $202.

These benefits are available for a wide variety of educational programs, from associate to graduate degrees at institutions from universities to vocational schools.

For more information, contact:
Department of Veterans
Central Office
Washington DC 20420
1-800-827-1000

Post-Vietnam Era Veterans Educational Assistance

More than $183 million is spent by the federal government each year to provide educational assistance to persons who served in the Armed Forces between 1977 and 1985.

Up to $8,100 worth of assistance per year is available to each recipient. They may also earn work study funds at minimum wage levels. Recipients may also get $1,200 a year to pay for tutorial assistance. The program is available to service personnel who made some contribution to the fund prior to April 1, 1987. The program matches $2 for every $1 that the recipient has paid into the fund.

> For more information, contact:
> Department of Veterans Affairs
> Central Office
> Washington DC 20420
> 1-800-827-1000

All-Volunteer Force Educational Assistance

This fund provides money for retired veterans who were honorably discharged to go back to school for professional or vocational education, and even covers correspondence courses. A maximum allowance of $12,600 per year is available. Work-study funds at minimum wage levels are available, and well as money for tutorial assistance.

This fund helps service personnel readjust to civilian life after they leave military service. For more information, contact:

> Department of Veterans Affairs
> Central Office
> Washington DC 20420
> 1-800-827-1000

Montgomery GI Bill

This fund provides educational assistance to service personnel who entered active duty for the first time after June 30, 1985. Those personnel who elected to join the program while on duty had a monthly deduction of $100 taken from their pay for the first 12 months of duty. They can now receive a cash payment of up to $14,998, all tax free.

Although a variety of eligibility restrictions apply, in general the fund is available to personnel who have been honorably discharged and have a high school diploma. Veterans who served on active duty for three years, or two years active duty plus four years in the Selected Reserve or National

Guard, receive $400 a month in basic benefits for three years. Under certain circumstances, the Veteran's Administration will enhance this with an additional bonus amount known as a "kicker."

Montgomery G.I. Bill benefits are also available to Selected Reservists who give a six year commitment. The educational benefit for them is $190 each month for three years.

For more information, contact:
Department of Veterans Affairs
Central Office
Washington DC 20420
1-800-827-1000

Chapter 7
Athletic Scholarships

I f you're thinking about college, you should be thinking about an athletic scholarship. Colleges have sports quotas to fill. And, they're looking for women! Now, at this point you might be saying to yourself, "Me? I'm not a big football star on my high school team, so why should any college give me an athletic scholarship?" Or if you're a woman, you might be thinking, "It's only the guys that get the sports scholarships, unless you're another Rebecca Lobo or Lisa Leslie."

Put these fables about athletic scholarships out of your mind right away! First of all, scholarships are available at all kinds of colleges and universities, large and small, for a wide variety of sports other than football and basketball. In addition to such better-known "secondary" sports as baseball, soccer, swimming, and track & field, many schools offer financial support for students who are skilled at such events as archery, badminton, cheerleading, and tennis.

Are you a great shot with a .22? Consider the possibility of a riflery scholarship. Love to be out on the water? How about a scholarship in sailing? Some schools even recruit athletes in such "fun" sports as water skiing and golf. Chances are, something you already do for recreation is considered a sport and might win you a scholarship to college if you do it well!

Also, don't worry if you're not the captain of your high school team, or if you're not setting local or state records in your chosen event. There are only a few "star" athletes to go around each year, and colleges have to fill out their annual incoming team rosters from the other dependable players who apply. If you show determination, commitment, and team spirit, you could be one of those students they select!

The Women's Advantage

Things have never been better in terms of the availability of sports scholarships for women. Congressional action on educational amendments and civil rights bills, and subsequent court decisions on those issues, have created a piece of legislation called "Title IX." This law was designed to create equal opportunities in athletics for female students, and it forbids sex discrimination in sports programs for any educational institution that receives federal funds.

One of the results of Title IX has been an explosion in the growth of new sports for women, designed to help colleges and universities meet their newly mandated goal of gender equity in their athletic departments. These emerging sports include such events as synchronized swimming, bowling, water polo, and women's crew.

If you show overall athletic ability and a firm dedication to give one of these sports "the old college try," you might even be awarded a scholarship in the sport without any prior experience at it! That's how eager most schools are to expand their women's athletics programs in order to fully comply with the terms of Title IX.

Hidden Benefits of Sports Scholarships

1. No Repayment

How much could an athletic scholarship mean to you, and to your college career? Obviously, the financial assistance could take a burden off you and your family. Even if you qualify for a student loan to cover your tuition or other educational expenses, that loan will someday have to be repaid, while a sports scholarship is a direct "gift," one that you'll never have to pay back.

This fact alone could make a great difference in your peace of mind and financial stability for years to come, even long after you've graduated from college. Your friends and fellow students who depended on college loans for their education will be working and scrimping for quite some time to repay what they owe — while you, on the other hand, with the benefit of an athletic scholarship during your college years, could start life in the "real world" free and clear, unencumbered by thousands of dollars in debts.

2. Prestige

There are other perks that come with a sports scholarship, not the least of which is the prestige and sense of gratification that your hard work and talent have been recognized and rewarded.

3. Extra Perks

Even before you get to campus, the fact that a college coach considers you potential material for an athletic scholarship can pay off in a big way. You'll have an influential advocate in the admissions process, a respected member of the college community who's telling the admissions committee, "This young man (or woman) deserves your special attention and consideration." Of course, this doesn't mean you can expect to slide by with a meager grade-point average or lousy SAT's; but it certainly can't hurt to have someone pulling for you when the tough admissions decisions are being made.

Come September, when you show up on campus for your freshman year, you'll be pleasantly surprised by how many extra advantages, big and small, are yours as the recipient of a sports scholarship. You're likely to be given special preference in terms of class selection, stepping to the head of the line in choosing popular classes and class times, as a way of accommodating your practice schedule. Overcrowded dormitories may seem to magically open up for you, the result of scarce housing space having been specifically set aside for student athletes.

You'll get preferential treatment in terms of advisors and counselors, too; the school has already acknowledged your special status, and the administration has made an investment in you and your success there. Rest assured that the faculty and staff will do whatever they can to help you make it through to graduation day with shining colors.

Types of Scholarships to Expect

Unless you're a real star athlete who's been actively recruited out of high school, you'll be awarded a partial scholarship rather than one which pays for every dime of your tuition, room and board, books, and other educational costs.

Every college or university has a certain maximum number of scholarships in particular sports at particular divisional levels that it is allowed to hand out each year. These limits are set by the collegiate athletic associations, such as the NCAA. For example, any Division I school that's a member of the NCAA (we'll explain the divisional breakdowns shortly) is permitted to grant 11.7 baseball scholarships per year, as compared to 85 football scholarships and 4.5 fencing scholarships. This doesn't mean the school has to award all those scholarships each and every year; only that it can't give more than that. The actual number available may vary from year to year, depending upon a school's budget and its strength or interest in that sport.

Note that four-year athletic scholarships are no longer awarded. Each year of your college career, your scholarship will come up for renewal, based on both academic and athletic performance.

Other Assistance

If you're offered a partial sports scholarship, and your family still can't handle the remaining educational expenses at the school of your choice, there are a variety of other ways you might be able to obtain additional financial assistance. See the rest of the education section in this book for details.

Insider's Tip:

Whatever your sport, get a coach to help you find the right sports scholarship for you!

Deciding if You Qualify

You've already seen that it's not necessary to be a star athlete in order to merit a sports scholarship; but there definitely are certain standards of quality and ability that you must meet in order to be considered a serious candidate for such an award.

You probably already have a pretty good idea of your own natural sports talents, and the degree to which you've managed to develop those skills. Make a list of your strengths and weaknesses as an athlete—your dedication to your sport, your physical prowess, your willingness to learn, your eagerness to win, your discipline to practice, your ability to excel on your own if you play an individual sport, and your dedication to the good of the group if yours is a team sport.

As honestly as you can, rate yourself on a scale of 1 to 10 on each of those factors, and as many more as you think are applicable to achieving excellence in your chosen sport. Take that list, and the ratings you've given yourself, to your high school coach, and ask him or her to review your own self-evaluation.

Tell your coach which schools you're thinking of applying to, and what amount of financial assistance you'll be seeking from them. Ask your coach to tell you frankly: does he or she think you have what it takes to compete on the college level, at the schools you're considering? Should you perhaps peg your expectations a little lower, say to a Division II school rather than Division I—or maybe even raise your hopes, and shoot for the stars?

Ask the same questions to anyone else you know who's qualified to assess your ability. Don't be afraid to seek the advice even of coaches on opposing teams; they've seen you play, probably more than once, and are likely to have made careful analysis of your skills as an opponent. If you have an older brother or sister, or family friend, who's already in college, ask them to rate you and how well they think you might perform as a college athlete.

Whether you've been actively recruited yourself or not, local area college coaches may well have been attending some of your high school games, scouting for talent. Ask your own coach to point them out to you, and introduce yourself to them. They'll admire you for asking their opinion of how you measure up. And, that personal contact may just pay off down the road, if you choose to apply to one of their schools.

Lastly, look to your stats. Every sport is a game of numbers, some more than others. Setting unrealistic expectations for yourself will lead only to disappointment. On the other hand, too much modesty and denial of your real talents is a waste. Create an honest picture of yourself in the mirror, believe what it tells you, and then act accordingly.

The Importance of Keeping Up Your Grades

Athletic scholarships are based on athletic skill, no question about it; but that certainly doesn't mean you should ignore your classwork in favor of ever greater glory and achievement on the playing field or in the gym. Far more so than in high school, college is about getting an education, and if you expect to have a successful four-year athletic career there, you'd better be prepared for some stiff academic challenges as well.

<u>Forget the stories you may have heard about student-athletes breezing right into college and coasting through without ever cracking a book;</u> if those days ever existed, they're long since gone. Today's college environment, like today's workplace, is more competitive than ever, and you'll be expected to pull your own weight grade-wise, regardless of your athletic accomplishments.

Getting into college in the first place is going to require a decent high school grade point average: the more prestigious the school, the higher the standard. Boneheads don't play for Princeton or for Stanford, not even if they have the athletic ability of a Tiger Woods or a Martina Hingis. Good grades will demonstrate that you have the discipline and the determination to succeed—important indications of your continued athletic performance as well as your academic proficiency.

If you're reading this in your freshman or sophomore year of high school, buckle down and concentrate on maintaining a good grade point average and class ranking, even as you focus on your athletic honors. If you're a junior or senior, and your grades haven't been all they should be, do everything you can to turn that around as quickly as possible. If a college admissions committee sees that you were able to learn and apply good work habits in your last year or two of high school, that might make the difference. However, it's far better to present them with a solid, stable record of unbroken academic effort.

There are, in fact, very specific and detailed regulations as to the high school grade performances of student-athletes who want to take part in collegiate athletic programs. These rules are constantly changing, and are far too complex to be reproduced here; ask your coach or your guidance counselor to see a copy of the annual publication "NCAA Guide for the College-Bound Student Athlete," and ask them to help you compare your own record to the current requirements.

Test scores also count for a lot, and it's never too soon or too late to start getting ready for the SAT or ACT tests. Studies have shown that concentrated "cram" courses do in fact aid students' results in these tests, even if it's only a matter of getting yourself accustomed to the way the questions are presented. If your school offers an SAT-prep course, by all means sign up for it; if not, look for private courses in your area, or purchase one of the many SAT preparatory books or CD-ROMS that are now on the market.

Choosing a College

There are three main intercollegiate athletic associations in the United States, designed to oversee and administer all aspects of intercollegiate sports. Student-athlete eligibility requirements, recruitment rules and procedures, and financial aid regulations all come under the jurisdiction of these associations. They are the NCAA (National Collegiate Athletic Association), the NAIA (National Association of Intercollegiate Athletics), and the NJCAA (National Junior College Athletic Association). Most colleges and universities belong to one of these organizations, though a few belong to other, less well-known associations.

Both the NCAA, with approximately 900 four-year-colleges, and the NJCAA, which represents over 500 two-year colleges, are broken down into three Divisions, numbered I, II, and III. The NAIA membership consists of about 400 four-year colleges, and it is split into Divisions I and II.

Generally speaking, in all three associations, Division I schools tend to be very competitive, are made up primarily of major colleges and universities, and offer a wide variety of athletic scholarships. Division II schools are somewhat less competitive, and some of them may be smaller than those in Division I, with fewer athletic scholarships awarded. In the NCAA and the NJCAA, Division III schools tend to be still smaller and less competitive than those in the first two divisions, and they award scholarships only on the basis of financial aid; no athletic scholarships are available.

NCAA Division I schools are the ones that get the most publicity in newspapers and on television, and the quality of their athletic programs is extremely high. However, you do not have to be an outstanding enough player to make it on a Division I team in order to get a sports scholarship. There are hundreds of excellent colleges in Division II, with exciting and competitive sports programs, respected academic credentials, and plenty of athletic scholarships to offer.

Selecting a College

Some of the general aspects you should pay attention to when selecting a school include:

- How far away it is from your home, and what that will mean in terms of travel expenses, homesickness, and cost of calling home regularly.

- Big city versus rural campus; both have their pluses and minuses, depending on your background and preferences.

- Social and cultural environment, which can vary dramatically from one part of the country to another.

- Weather and climate; if you grew up on the Gulf Coast, it might be hard to get used to winters in upstate New York, for example.

- Recreational opportunities on and off campus.

- Coed or single-sex school.

- Ethnic and cultural diversity of the student body.

- Academic difficulty.

- Cost of tuition and living, over and above what your scholarship may provide.

- Whether the school offers classes or majors in your non-athletic fields of interest.

Check Out Your Final Choices

If you're going to be attending a college on a sports scholarship, you'll definitely want to take a close look at its athletic department before you commit yourself to attending. Some of the questions you might want to consider and compare for each of the schools on your list would be:

- How much time would you be expected to commit to your sport: how many hours a day of practice, how long is the season?

- What's the coaching staff like? Do you respect them, could you get along well with them?

- What sort of athletic facilities does the school have, and how well do they maintain them?

- Does the athletic department adequately support your particular sport, or is it considered of minor importance to the school?

- What's the level of competition you would face? Could you hold your own, and make a worthwhile contribution to your sport or team?

- Does the athletic department actively encourage its student-athletes to excel in academics as well as on the field?

Don't Wait to be Discovered!

Too many high school athletes think that all they have to do is perform well in their local area, and college coaches from all over the country will come flocking to recruit them. Well, that's just not the case!

Scouting is an expensive and time-consuming proposition for college coaches, and only the very top high school "name" players are actively sought out. Most of the qualified high school athletes, even the very good ones who could be eligible for major scholarships, will have to bring themselves to the attention of the coaching staff at the schools they want to attend.

The first thing you'll want to do is compile a resume of your sports history, just as you'd prepare a resume of your work history if you were applying for a job. In a very real sense, that's exactly what you are doing: you're offering to labor hard and long at your sport, which will profit the college through paid attendance or publicity for its athletic events. The school, your potential "employer," will be paying you for your efforts by providing you with a free or low-cost education.

Your resume should have your name, address, and phone number at the top, and it should include brief details as to your personal, athletic, and academic background. Keep it simple; don't write whole paragraphs about your sports triumphs, just make a line-by-line listing of the following:

- Teams or events in which you've participated through your high school career

- The stats and standings achieved

- The various awards and honors you or you team have received.

The academic side should include the following:

- Your grade point average and class standing

- All relevant test scores such as SAT and ACT

- Any academic honors you may have been awarded.

For the personal information, focus on positive aspects such as:

- Community service projects in which you may have been involved

- Jobs you've held

- Membership in school or extracurricular organizations.

The resume should be no more than two pages long, neatly typewritten, and it should conclude with the names, addresses, and phone numbers of three or four references—coaches or athletic directors who are familiar with you and your abilities.

Once you've compiled your resume, you'll want to compose a cover letter to go along with it. If writing isn't your strong suit, get a parent, a teacher, or a coach to help you do the letter. A sample cover letter might look something like this:

Ms. Cathy Wheeler
Head Women's Swimming Coach
Burdine College
Department of Athletics
56888 College Blvd.
Watsonville, Ind.

Dear Ms. Wheeler:

My name is Rachel Travers, and I am a member of the swim team at North Pembroke High School in Lincoln, Delaware, where I will soon complete my junior year. I am very interested in both the academic and the swim programs at Burdine College, and would very much appreciate any further information you might be able to send me. I would also like to know more about the availability of athletic scholarships at Burdine.

Enclosed please find my sports resume, along with other materials which should give you a good idea of my academic and athletic background. If you would like to see a videotape of my performance in several recent swim meets, I would be happy to send that to you as well.

I expect to be visiting the Burdine campus sometime this summer, and would like to meet with you in person if that's possible. If you will be available, please let me know what dates would be convenient for you, and I can arrange my schedule accordingly.

Thank you for your time and consideration. I look forward to hearing from you.

Sincerely,

Rachel Travers

> **Insider's Tip:**
>
> You will be first judged by the quality of your letter. Use a computer — from the library or your parent's office if you don't have one of your own — to type your letter and your personal essay.

Checklist Before Mailing

Now put together a package that contains the following:

- Your cover letter on top

- Your sports resume beneath it

- A photograph of yourself

- Your letters of recommendation from coaches and teachers

- Any news clippings you may have about your achievements in your sport.

Use a large paper clip to keep all the pages together (do not fold any of them), place them in a large manila envelope, and take it to the post office to make sure it goes out with sufficient postage.

Follow-Up

After you've sent this introductory package off to the college coach, wait no more than a couple of weeks to hear back from him or her. If you haven't received a reply by then, check back with a note or phone call inquiring whether the coach received your letter and resume. Don't be afraid to be politely persistent in your follow-ups; such determination shows you're serious about your sport and about your interest in the school, and will help keep your name foremost in the coach's mind when he or she begins deciding which high school athletes to recruit for the college's program.

If you're going to be competing in an area where the college coach might be willing to come and watch your performance, by all means let them know this, and invite them to attend the game or meet. You might also ask your high school coach to call the college on your behalf; or, if you happen to know any alumni or former players from the college you are interested in, they might be willing to put in a good word for you. Don't be shy about promoting yourself. Remember: the squeaky wheel gets the grease!

If you do have the opportunity to visit the campus of the college you're interested in, pay attention to every aspect of the school and its environment. This may be your new home for four years or more, and you want to make sure it's to your liking.

When you do meet the college coach, be yourself. If they're seeing you in person, that means they're already interested in you to some degree, and you should feel free to exhibit a relaxed, confident attitude. This is someone who may be your friend and mentor for your whole college career; let down your guard a bit, and let them see the human side of you, even as you're making your own decision about whether you'd feel comfortable working closely with them for several years to come.

A Few Words of Caution

The college athletic associations have some very strict and specific rules about contact between high school athletes and college coaches. If you or the coach violate any of these recruiting regulations, it could mean serious trouble for either or both of you. Contact your high school coach or guidance counselor for the latest details on these complex rules.

Finally, if and when you do get a scholarship offer, get it in writing, and don't make any hard and fast decisions until you've had a chance to review the terms of the offer with your family and other adult advisors.

Good luck, and go for the gold!

Chapter 8
Other Sources of
Financial Aid

1. State Programs

Each state offers its own array of grants, scholarships, loans and fee reductions. However, these are usually reserved for students in that state who attend state universities. It's estimated that more than $1 billion is available in state-sponsored aid each year.

At least 20 states offer their students financial incentives to stay in their home state to go to college. The best place to get information about aid in specific states is from state agencies or commissions of higher education. You will find the phone numbers for these agencies listed by state in *Free Cash Grants, Vol. 2* under Appendix A. This Appendix lists scholarships by state that are available from both state agencies and private foundations.

Other sources of information about state grants are your high school and college counselors. The federal FAFSA form has a box which can be checked if you are interested in receiving state aid. Check it! For more information, phone the Federal Student Aid Information Center at 1-800-433-3243.

Insider's Tip:

We have all heard how expensive it is to go to college out of state. What most students don't realize is that many states offer exchange programs. These programs will allow you to "switch" states with another student so you can attend an out-of-state school at little or no extra cost. Check to see if this program is offered in your state.

2. Private Foundations

Although they are often harder to find than federal or state sources, private sources of grants and scholarships can often be very lucrative. They are also advantageous because there is less bureaucracy involved. Many times, this aid comes in the form of direct, no-strings-attached grants, the best kind of student aid you can get. This is especially true for families who don't qualify for need-based federal aid.

Some type of scholarship is offered by almost all of America's biggest corporations. The most famous are the Coca-Cola, Tylenol, and Westinghouse scholarships. But even smaller hometown businesses, churches, and service organizations offer financial aid—everyone from the Elks Lodge to the Veterans Associations.

There are many ways to search out the scholarships. A good place to start is Appendix A in *Free Cash Grants Vol. 2*, which has many sources of foundation scholarships listed by state.

3. Individual Colleges

In order to entice qualified students, many colleges and universities offer their own scholarships. These can vary from waivers of tuition and housing costs to student jobs and loans. In fact, about 20 percent of the student aid that is awarded each year comes directly from colleges and universities!

Because colleges are more interested than ever in attracting a diverse and top-notch student body, they are offering more merit-based scholarships than ever before. Many of these scholarships can be extremely generous. <u>In fact, schools have been known to offer a full waiver of tuition and fees to certain students as long as they keep their grade point average around 3.5!</u>

The best way to find out about these programs is to call the specific schools that you are interested in attending. Pick a wide range of schools. Many times, schools that are regarded as particularly expensive and hard to get into will offer the best individual scholarships. Don't be afraid to check them out!

On the next page you will find a sample letter to send to colleges for more information about their academic and financial aid programs.

VIA FIRST CLASS MAIL

TODAY'S DATE

Director of Admissions

SCHOOL NAME

SCHOOL ADDRESS

Dear Director:

I am interested in attending (NAME OF SCHOOL) and I will be graduating from high school in (YEAR). Please send me a brochure, a freshman application, and any other information that would help me learn more about your school.

Please also send me information about financial aid and housing opportunities.

Thank you very much.

Sincerely,

(YOUR NAME)

(YOUR ADDRESS)

Insider's Tip:

Many official financial aid forms ask the student if their name and personal information can be released to scholarship programs. Always answer "yes"! Programs such as the National Merit Scholarship Corporation rely on this information for identifying students who are eligible for their programs.

4. AmeriCorps

At a White House ceremony in 1994, President Clinton officially launched AmeriCorps, which was hailed as a domestic Peace Corps. This was good news for a number of needy communities who receive help from a qualified corps of enthusiastic young workers. It's also good news for college students, because it allows them to get valuable experience by doing good deeds, PLUS money for college.

Students typically serve a term of one or two years directly after they get out of high school. They take community service jobs that range from helping to fight youth violence in Jacksonville, Florida to training migrant workers to avoid pesticide poisoning in Ohio.

In return for their service, students receive a living allowance of $7,500 per year and an educational allowance of $4,725 for each year that they serve. Students may also serve part time and earn $2,362 per year. AmeriCorps workers only get the money once they are actually enrolled in a college.

For more information or an application, call 1-800-94-ACORPS and ask for the AmeriCorps National Referral Form. The AmeriCorps headquarters is located at 1201 New York Ave. NW, Washington, DC 20525.

5. Upward Bound

This is a program which reaches out to low-income families. In most of these families, no one has even gone to college. The goal of the program is to change that pattern. Upward Bound aims to help young people from families who know very little about college to rise "upward" into a college education.

The Upward Bound program provides instruction to high school students in order to help them be prepared for college. But it is more than just a tutorial service. In addition to instruction in reading, writing and study skills, the program offers academic, financial and personal counseling. In addition, participants in the program are exposed to cultural events and academic programs that will help them become aware of college and the rewards they will find there.

Upward Bound also strives to keep the students informed about college education opportunities. This includes getting them ready for college entrance exams. It also includes helping them request and complete financial aid applications.

To be eligible for the program, students must have completed the 8th grade, be between the ages of 13 and 19 (except veterans) and show a need for academic support. All students must be either from low-income families or be potential first-generation college students. Students are recommended by local teachers, social workers, or clergy.

A total of 600 of these awards was given in 1996. The program is administered by the Federal Office of Higher Education Program. For more information, phone (202) 708-4804.

Financial Aid Letters

Should you ever need a letter to request more information about financial aid (and you most certainly will!), you can use the sample letter on this page. Use this letter when you request more information about the scholarship listings in *Free Cash Grants Vol. 2*. Always include a self-addressed, stamped envelope.

You now have dozens of different paths to choose to find money for college. The financial aid you need is well within your reach. All you have to do is start your search. Do it today! We have nothing but confidence in your success!

Sample Letter To Request Information About Grants And Loans

VIA FIRST CLASS MAIL

TODAY' DATE

(NAME OF SCHOLARSHIP SOURCE)

(ADDRESS)

Dear Sir or Madam:

Please forward an application and any information or guidelines you have regarding your financial aid program for higher education. I have enclosed a self-addressed, stamped envelope.

Sincerely,

(YOUR NAME)

(YOUR ADDRESS)

Chapter 9
Getting Ready for Success

It's been said that the ultimate job is doing something you love that earns all the money you need. For many people, that means owning and operating their own business. If you're thinking about starting your own business, congratulations! Many people dream of being their own boss and having the freedom to choose how and when and where they will work—but too few people actually take the plunge.

The chapters in the Business section of this book will help you get out of the starting gate, whether you're a brand new entrepreneur or a seasoned business owner with dreams of developing and expanding your business. There are countless resources at the Federal, State, and local level to help you realize your dreams—from free business counseling and research to free cash grants and low-interest loans. You'll also learn about the Small Business Administration and what it can do for you, plus tips on finding venture capital and private investors for your business.

See the listings in *Free Cash Grants Vol. 2* for sources of cash grants and loans. Meanwhile, the information in the next few chapters will give you the know-how you need to move forward with your business plans. We've got lots of ground to cover. So here we go!

The Entrepreneurial Factor

So you want to start your own business! Before you begin, the first question you need to ask yourself is this: Do I have a burning desire to be successful in my own independent business? Studies of businesses have shown a direct connection between a business owner's personal commitment and their financial success. In other words—if you want to make it badly enough, chances are you will!

To help you decide whether starting your own business is right for you, take the short quiz on the next page.

Self-Employment Aptitude Test	YES	NO
1. Do I have lots of energy?	_____	_____
2. Am I in good physical health?	_____	_____
3. Am I able to work long hours?	_____	_____
4. Do I have special skills in my chosen business endeavor?	_____	_____
5. Do I like to plan ahead, set goals and see that my plans are carried out?	_____	_____
6. Am I ready to take some risks?	_____	_____
7. Do I have leadership qualities?	_____	_____
8. Do I have a sense of humor?	_____	_____
9. Am I flexible and adaptable?	_____	_____
10. Do I thrive on change and make changes easily?	_____	_____

Entrepreneurs are self-confident, hard-working, energetic, determined RISK TAKERS; they have a need to achieve and a desire for independence. Most entrepreneurs are innovators. They are people with big ideas (and often with little money) who are so excited about their business that they JUST DO IT. They include the self-employed, "independent contractors" and machine repair shops; insurance agents, tax preparers, physicians, and attorneys; they are franchise operators, salespeople and small shopkeepers. Often they are home-based "moonlighters" earning a bit extra money in their off-work hours.

People start their own businesses for many reasons. They seek financial independence, new career opportunities, or a flexible work schedule. Or, they want to be their own boss or create a new product, advance a new idea, or gamble on the possibility of big money.

Does this sound like you? Then CONGRATULATIONS, you are on the way to building a SUCCESSFUL BUSINESS STRATEGY and a PLAN of ACTION that will bring you many profitable returns!

Getting Started

Your business success depends on a number of factors. To begin with, you must know your competition, your market, your business, AND your customers. You must be able to react to changes and stay competitive in the marketplace.

Because our work world and the global economy are changing so rapidly, it is more important than ever for small business owners to build a strong foundation by learning the basics. You need to know how to finance your business endeavors, how to make your business profitable, when to use consultants, who to hire (and who NOT to hire), and where to find answers to your questions.

<u>One of the best ways to get started is to take business courses in your area.</u> Most community colleges, adult education programs, and local business schools offer courses in the basics of starting and running your own business. If you are a true "do-it-yourselfer," you might want to add the following books to your library:

How To Start Your Own Business, Keep Your Own Books, Pay Your Taxes, And Stay Out Of Trouble, by Bernard Kamaroff, CPA; ISBN 0-917510-10-2; 190 pg paperback; includes a year supply of ledger worksheets and valuable information on permits, licenses, financing and insurance.

The Entrepreneur Magazine Small Business Advisor, a one-stop information source for starting, managing, and growing a small business; John Wiley & Sons, Inc. 1995; ISBN 0-471-10988-6 (hardcover), ISBN 0-471-10989 (paperback). Over 600 pages packed with expert knowledge on market research, business plans, franchising, financing, managing, and other topics.

Small Business Resource Guide, Braddock Communications, 1996. Discusses effective planning and the right kind of financing for your business venture. Available from the U.S. Chamber of Commerce, 1-800-638-6582.

> **Insider's Tip:**
>
> If you have unlimited money available, you can hire experts to help you with some aspects of your business. But most small businesspeople find it's better to save their money by hiring out the work in one or two areas (like hiring a bookkeeper) and running the other areas of their business themselves.

A Business In Your Home

If you want to work at home, the good news is you can start a home-based business with very little cash investment. You can make or sell products such as balloon-o-grams for party shops, custom lampshades for decorators, wedding cakes, patchwork quilts, or mail order tool kits. If your skills are service oriented, you can provide accounting, advertising, grant writing, convention planning, home health care, research, tutoring or word processing—ALL FROM THE COMFORT AND CONVENIENCE OF YOUR HOME.

There are some real advantages to working from your home.

- Low overhead. Use a spare room or garage.

- Flexible schedule. Work around the family schedule. If you are a night owl, you can work when your kids are sleeping.

- Save on cost of clothing (no need to Dress for Success) and meals out. You can grab a snack whenever you want!

- You can often price your product or service to beat your competitors and still make a profit.

If you do decide to operate a business in your home, you'll have plenty of company. There are more people working out of their homes nationwide than ever before. Small is beautiful! According to the U.S. Department of Commerce, nearly 90% of all businesses in the U.S. have fewer than 10 employees.

Be sure to check your local city or county regulations. Get whatever licenses you need and pay the required fees to be legal. And check with a tax accountant so you can take advantage of the home office deduction and other tax advantages of working from home!

Getting Money For Your New Business

Most new businesses are underfinanced, but don't let that stop you. Lots of successful businesses have started on a shoestring. The key is to make sure you have enough cash to cover your basic living expenses at all times. That might mean holding on to your regular job a while longer, or getting a part-time job for now just to make sure you can keep up with your bills while you build your business.

Then, of course, there are all kinds of grants and loans you can get to help you start or grow your business. The first step is to decide exactly how much you need. Begin with an estimate of all your expenses, including start up costs, equipment, supplies, promotion, and first-year operating expenses. Then double the estimate. That is a safe amount.

A general rule of thumb is that current assets (cash & equipment) should be worth twice your current liabilities. For example, let's say you are going to start a cake decorating business and you need $4,500 for a stove, utensils, supplies, insurance, and brochures. Try to cover $3,000 of this total from your own cash or cash grants, and you can borrow the remaining $1,500. When you use this rule, your debts never get so high that they threaten the existence of your business.

Your Personal Balance Sheet

When you go to bankers or other lenders to get a loan for your business—or when you apply to agencies that offer free cash grants—they will ask to see a balance sheet for your business that shows your net worth. You can make your own balance sheet by using the form on the next page to list all of your assets (what you own) and your liabilities (what you owe).

ASSETS	LIABILITIES
_____ Cash on hand	_____ Current bills
_____ Checking account balance	_____ Home mortgage
_____ Savings accounts	_____ Auto loans
_____ Real Estate (current market value)	_____ Other bank loans
_____ Autos, trucks, equipment	_____ Credit card balances
_____ Stocks & bonds	_____ Other debts
_____ Insurance cash value	
_____ Other assets	
_____ **TOTAL ASSETS**	_____ **TOTAL LIABILITIES**

When you finish your lists, add up all the assets, subtract your liabilities, and you will have your NET WORTH.

Your Credit History

Next, bankers, lenders, and agencies that give free cash grants will want to look at your credit history. They will want to know: Do you pay your bills on time? Do your liabilities exceed your assets? Is there a collection agency on your tail? Do you owe back taxes?

Prospective lenders are interested in your credit history because it gives them important clues about you and the future of your business. If you are 'living within your means' it's a good indicator that you can manage your business finances wisely, too. So before you submit a grant or loan application to a bank, lender, or other funding agency, be prepared by requesting a copy of your credit report. Every credit bureau gets their data from one of three information agencies: Experian (formerly TRW), Trans Union, or Equifax. You can request a copy of your credit report by calling them at the numbers listed below:

Experian: 1-800-831-5614

Trans Union: (312) 408-1400

Equifax: (770) 375-2585

It usually takes about 30 days to receive your report in the mail. If you find that your credit report lists errors—for example, accounts you have paid that are still listed as unpaid—it's up to you to set the record straight. Supply the facts to the credit agency in writing. Be sure you have the proof to back up your claim—the agency won't investigate if they think your claim is "frivolous."

If possible, get credit reports from at least two different sources. This will give you the same information that the bank, lender, or grantmaking agency will have as soon as you apply for a loan or grant. Also, it will allow you to correct any errors in the report or write a memo to explain unusual circumstances.

Insider's Tip:

Another easy way to get a copy of your credit report is to call a nearby department store and ask which credit bureau they use. Then call the credit bureau and ask for a copy of your credit report.

Market Research: Your Ace in the Hole

Before you sit down to write a business plan, you'll need to conduct some market research. Along with a description of your product, your business plan needs to include a description of your competition, as well as an estimate of your potential market share.

Market research helps you identify your short term goals, develop plans and objectives, and suggest different approaches to meet those goals. You need to know who your competitors are, how much demand there is for your product, and how to price your goods or services to compete successfully.

Researching your competition is the first step. What are the strengths and weaknesses of the competitors in your market? Which firms are successful, and why? When you have the answers to these questions, you'll be able to develop a successful market strategy to sell your product or service.

Researching your customers is the next step. Who are your potential customers? Where are they located? How much will they pay for your product or service? What is the demand for your product or service, and how can you increase the demand? Is the market growing or shrinking? How can you attract customers to your business?

Sources of Market Research Data

- Start at your local library. Look in trade association listings and journals.

- Check local and regional business associations (Chambers of Commerce) for annual reports and membership lists (potential customers).

- Talk to insurance representatives, bankers and real estate professionals.

- Study economic forecasts for your area.

- Look in the phone book under headings related to your business.

Conduct Your Own Customer Survey

It's a great idea to do market research by conducting your own customer survey. Develop a series of questions that relate to your business. Then call people in your area who are prospective customers and do a brief telephone survey.

For example, say that you want to sell computerized mailing lists. Here's a sample of how your phone survey might go:

"Hi, my name is Pat. I am conducting a survey of local users of computer generated mailing lists. Could you tell me if you have ever purchased such a list? If it was priced at x$ would you buy one? How often do you need such lists? When was the last time you bought one? From whom? Were you satisfied with the service they provided? If you could give them any suggestions to serve you better, what would they be?"

You get the idea. The more information you can gather about your potential customers' needs AND about your competitors, the farther ahead you will be.

Keep detailed notes for all your research. You can use 3" X 5" cards, a standard notebook, or your computer. File your research under topic headings like Competitors, Potential Customers, Price Ranges, Areas for Potential Business, etc.

Now that you have your credit history in hand, and you've completed market research on your competition and your customers, you're ready to start writing a business plan!

Why Write A Business Plan?

A business plan is your number-one resource when it comes it getting financing for your business! When you approach banks, lenders, and grantmaking agencies to get grants and loans, the first thing they'll ask to see is a business plan. Not only that, but the process of putting together a business plan forces you to take an objective look at your business as a whole. You can learn things about your business that you never knew before!

Don't hire a consultant to prepare your plan. Do it yourself. If you need help, consult SCORE volunteers in your community. It's FREE! (SCORE stands for the Service Corps of Retired Executives, a service sponsored by the SBA. For more details, see the next chapter.)

Your business plan will explain the proposed activities and specific needs of your business. It's both a blueprint to build your business, and an outline to grow your business. We can't emphasize it enough: without an adequate business plan, you won't be able to get the financing you need to make your business successful.

Once you've got your business plan in place, use it! It will help you get started and stay on the path to success.

Insider's Tip:

Lots of competition does not guarantee that there's a market for your product, BUT it should not scare you away. Often, if there are many successful people in the business it shows that there's even more business to be had!

Outline For Your Business Plan

1. Begin with your product. Briefly describe your goods or services.

2. Report your market data. List competitive features of your product, such as size, weight, durability, convenience, quality, price, customer service, etc. For a service business, list your experience, references, and unique qualities. What needs will your product or service satisfy? How will it be used? Who will buy it? Compare your product or service to the State of the Art. Why is yours better?

3. Analyze your major competitors. Who else sells similar products? Evaluate their strengths, weaknesses, estimated market share and profitability. Here you need to focus on how you will cope with your competitors and what plans you have to build on their weaknesses and challenge their strengths.

4. Estimate the total market share your business will capture. Develop market forecast and measurement of market share. Identify market trends, volume and profit goals. List potential customers with an estimate of annual business from each.

5. Pricing. Figure out how much to charge. Will you use a sliding scale? Variable rates? Beat a competitor's price? Explain your choice of pricing and project an annual growth rate for sales.

6. Describe your marketing strategy. Tell how you will identify and classify potential clients/customers. Which market segments will you pursue? What promotional methods will you use? Where will you advertise? How will you spend advertising dollars? How will your products/services be distributed—point of sale, direct mail, direct sales, wholesale/distributors? What will be the terms of sale? How will you ensure performance and customer satisfaction?

7. Include the following financial data:

- ASSETS available to the business (inventory, equipment, cash, etc.)

- CASH FLOW PROJECTIONS for the first three years. Show your operating budget projections, month by month. How will you receive and spend your business income?

- PROFIT AND LOSS STATEMENT for past three years, and projections for next three years. Use low level, mid level, and "exceeds expectations" estimates.

• DETAILED BUDGET and projected sources and amounts of revenue.

• BEGINNING BALANCE SHEET for a new business.

• WRITTEN CREDIT REPORTS and REFERENCES.

• TAX RETURNS for the past three years.

You're On Your Way!

This chapter has taken you through the basics of getting ready to obtain free cash grants and loans for your business. Now you're ready to learn about the programs that can lend you a helping hand! In the next few chapters, you'll learn about the SBA, Federal and State grant programs, foundation grants, corporate grants, and other sources of money for your business. Read on, and make it happen!

Chapter 10
All About The SBA

The SBA, or Small Business Administration, is a Federal agency that started in the 1950s to help develop small businesses. Today, there are over 4,000 SBA employees working in branch offices nationwide. The SBA does it all, from lending money to operating a telephone hotline to answer your business questions (1-800-UASK-SBA).

The fact is, small businesses make up nearly 99% of all businesses in this country, and they provide jobs for more than half the working people in the U.S.! Small businesses continue to create the vast majority of new jobs. And millions of businesses would not exist today without the help of SBA loans. In 1995, the SBA granted loans to 38,400 small businesses for a total of more than $7.4 BILLION dollars!

In addition to loans, the SBA is big on providing free information and other help to small businesses. Over 100 SBA field offices nationwide offer workshops, individual counseling, videotapes, and publications. There is a list of SBA Field Offices at the end of this chapter.

This chapter will describe the many services offered to small businesses by the SBA. Be sure to take advantage of these great opportunities—you'll be glad you did!

Insider's Tip

The SBA will send you a FREE business start-up kit that includes valuable information on financing, management and consulting services. Call the SBA Hotline at 1-800-UASK-SBA.

SBA Business Information Centers (BIC)

Throughout the country, you'll find libraries of information on small business at your disposal at SBA Business Information Centers. Here you can learn about the latest computer equipment for your business, get help with market research through interactive videos and databases, use the latest spreadsheet and planning software, and prepare graphic presentations. Most services are free of charge. There is a complete list of BIC offices at the end of this chapter.

Service Corps of Retired Executives (SCORE)

SCORE is one of the best resources around for small businesses. In 1997, over 12,500 retired executives volunteered their time through SCORE to offer FREE, one-on-one business counseling for new entrepreneurs and small business owners.

SCORE's successful businesspeople are the voice of experience, providing planning and problem-solving expertise. They also present management, financing and business workshops and seminars—plus training in accounting, market analysis, site selection, trade promotion and other specialized topics. Advice on hiring consultants and other professional services is available on request.

SCORE's mentors are the core of SBA technical assistance. You will find them through the BICs listed at the end of this chapter. For a list of SCORE members in your area, contact: SCORE, 409 Third St. SW, 6th Floor, Washington DC 20024; or call 1-800-634-0245; or find them on the World Wide Web at http://www.sbaonline.sba.gov/score.

Insider's Tip

The SBA Office of Advocacy researches the effect federal policies have on small firms and assists owners in getting around red tape in government programs. Ten regional advocates monitor legislative proposals and business trends. You can learn more about this quiet, behind-the-scenes lobbying group by checking their website at http://www.sbaonline.sba.gov/gopher.

Small Business Investment Companies (SBICs)

Congress created Small Business Investment Companies to help entrepreneurs obtain start-up financing. Privately owned investment firms, licensed and regulated by the SBA, use a combination of their own money and government funds for venture capital. Some SBICs will fund new or start-up businesses; others will invest only in companies with a proven track record in certain fields. They also provide management assistance, since they hope to prosper as the business becomes successful.

More than 200 SBIC offices are located throughout the country. See the next chapter for details on the application process and eligiblity requirements for SBIC assistance.

Office of Women's Business Ownership (OWBO)

This office provides assistance for women-owned businesses. The OWBO offers technical, financial, and management information, business workshops, and help getting SBA loans. No grants are available. Their mentoring program is called WNET (Women's Network for Entrepreneurial Training). It pairs up experienced women business owners with new women entrepreneurs to help start and grow their businesses.

For more information about this group or to find other resources or publications available through OWBO, (including locations of all 54 Womens Business Centers nationwide), check their homepage at http:/www.sbaonline.sba.gov/womeninbusiness or call them at (202) 205-6673.

SBIR (Small Business Innovative Research)

The SBA coordinates the Federal SBIR program, or Small Business Innovative Research. Small, for-profit businesses with fewer than 500 employees are eligible for SBIR funding. Competition is keen; only one out of every ten projects is funded during Phase I. Most of these projects are innovative.

SBIR funds are meant to create new technology and provide opportunities and incentives for businesses to convert research into commercial products. Eleven federal agencies participate in this program administered through the SBA. The most frequent participants are the Departments of Defense, Commerce, Energy, Health & Human Services and the Environmental Protection Agency. See the next chapter for more information on how to apply for these funds.

SBIR awards are available in three phases:

Phase I – Project Feasibility. A maximum of $50,000 is available for up to 6 months.

Phase II – Principal Research Effort. SBIR may lend up to $500,000 for 2 years.

Phase III – Commercial Development. Usually this phase is funded through a venture capital firm or large corporation.

Small Business Development Centers (SBDC)

Small Business Development Centers provide counseling, training, and other technical assistance through nearly 1,000 District offices located across the country. Small businesses may obtain assistance from the SBDC as long as they cannot afford to pay a private consultant. Services include economic development and international trade assistance; engineering, production, and procurement advice; feasibility studies; and management and financial information. While these centers are directed by the SBA, much of their funding comes from State and local sources.

What Else Does The SBA Do?

The SBA does not often make direct loans to small business. What it does do is make loan guarantees to banks. This means that small businesses can borrow money from local banks, EVEN WHEN THEY MIGHT NOT MEET THE USUAL LENDING REQUIREMENTS. The SBA will guarantee up to 75% of loan amounts from commercial banks up to a maximum of $750,000.

The main reasons banks usually turn down business loans is either because business owners don't have enough experience in their chosen venture, or because business owners don't have enough of their own money to invest in the venture. SBA loan guarantees are a way of getting around these problems. If you have a solid business plan, a track record, and some collateral, you shouldn't have any trouble qualifying for a SBA guaranteed loan. Contact your nearest SBA Field Office for help with loan guarantees (see the list at the end of this chapter).

Are You Eligible For an SBA Guaranteed Loan?

If you can answer yes to the following questions, you are eligible for an SBA guaranteed loan:

1. Are you a business that is independently owned and operated for a profit?

2. Do you need money for working capital, equipment, inventory, supplies, buildings or land, or to establish a line of credit?

3. Have you been turned down by your local bank or lending institution?

4. Can you supply a business plan and a statement showing how you will repay the loan?

5. Will you agree to comply with SBA regulations about nondiscrimination in employment or services?

The following organizations are NOT eligible for loan guarantees from the SBA: non-profit organizations, academic schools, banks or brokerage firms, gambling casinos, newspapers and magazines, real estate speculators, and service companies with income over certain limits.

If you have questions about your eligibility, call the SBA field office in your area. (See the list at the end of this chapter.) Here are a few general rules to remember:

• Before you apply for a loan, you should get a credit check. Contact a credit bureau in your area to find out how your creditors view you as a financial risk. See Chapter 9 for how to get a copy of your credit report.

• Most SBA loans are for $100,000 to $750,000. The SBA does not usually lend less than $50,000, but there are exceptions. For example, see the LowDoc Loan Program described below.

• SBA expects you to make a reasonable financial investment. That means a personal contribution of at least 20-50% of your projected costs.

• There are specific requirements for the use of the money you borrow. See the restrictions below, or contact the SBA for details.

What Can You Do With Money You Borrow From SBA?

YOU CAN:

• Provide working capital for your business

• Buy supplies, machinery or inventory

• Use the money to establish a line of credit for seasonal product inventory (like buying Easter baskets and bunnies in the Fall for Spring production)

• Buy land or buildings

• Expand existing faciliies

YOU CANNOT:

• Pay back taxes to the IRS

• Use the money for investment purposes

• Use the money to repay debt

• Use the money for gambling endeavors

Loans & Technical Assistance Offered by the SBA

The SBA offers technical assistance and several types of loans to meet the needs of small businesses.

THE BASIC - 7(a) Regular Business Loan

90% of all loans guaranteed by SBA are the SBA 7(a). This basic loan guarantee program is for expansion, renovation, purchase of equipment, land or buildings, working capital or inventory. Loans are provided through private lenders to small businesses that otherwise could not secure financing on reasonable terms. The maximum amount that can be guaranteed is generally $750,000, but there are occasional exceptions. The average loan guarantee in this category is close to $200,000.

SECTION 8 (a) - Technical Assistance Program

This is a business development program for socially and economically disadvantaged individuals and small firms located in areas of high unemployment. Specialized management training, services, loans, and assistance in marketing are some of the services available. Through grants, government contracts, and agreements, the SBA can guarantee work for participants as subcontractors for many federal agencies. To be eligible, the firm must be at least 51% owned by an individual who qualifies as a socially or economically disadvantaged citizen or who is a Native American.

Low Documentation Loan Program (Low Doc)

This program relies on the strength of an individual's credit history and character. It is a simple one-page application available for loan requests of less than $50,000. For businesses seeking $50,000 to $100,000, tax returns for the previous three years and additional financial statements are required. Monies may be used for the same purposes as the BASIC 7(a) loan.

FA$TRAK Pilot Program

This is a program designed to help people borrow up to $100,000 (with 50% guaranteed by SBA) for start-up cost of a new business. Local lenders offer these loans to small businesses in their communities with no added paperwork, and no waiting for SBA approvals. Loans can usually be approved within one week.

MICRO-LOAN Demonstration Program

Under this program, the SBA makes money available to local non-profit organizations which then loan it to local businesses that need very small ($100 to $25,000) amounts of money for short periods of time. Loans average $10,000; they are made at competitive interest rates and can be used to buy supplies, inventory, equipment, furniture, or for working capital. Like FA$TRAK, these loans can generally be processed within a week.

Suggestions for Getting Help from the SBA

DO:

- Call 1-800-8 ASK-SBA before you apply for a loan

- Call the SBA hotline before you start to write your business plan.

- Find a mentor through SCORE

DON'T:

- Expect the SBA to fund a business in which you do not have a personal investment

- Overlook other sources for financing and growing your business

Components of an Effective Loan Proposal

If you'd like to apply for one of the loans described above, first call the SBA Hotline for details, or contact a local lender to see if they handle these SBA programs. Then, you're ready to roll!

First and foremost, a winning loan proposal is neat, well organized, and concise. Be sure you submit the proposal with ample time for review. Last-minute pleas for help make you look scattered and disorganized to a lender. The proposal must also be complete, containing all of the following:

- Brief summary explaining your business

- Purpose, amount, and type of loan you need

- Proposed schedule for repayment (show at least two sources or alternatives for payment of the loan)

- Collateral you will provide for the loan

- Organization chart showing guarantors, owner(s) and management of your company; include description of compensation and benefit package

- Short term (1-3 years) and long term (3-5 years) projections of your financial needs; include profit projections and assumptions

- Three basic Financial Statements

- Balance Sheet: current and from previous three fiscal year-end reports

- Income Statements (Profit & Loss) for the past three years

- Cash Flow Projections: List of revenues and expenses (month by month) for first three years, showing how you will repay the loan

- Documentation of appropriate insurance coverage

- Background information about your business, resumes of key personnel, assets, liabilities, tax returns for past three years

- Your Business Plan

Writing Your Loan Proposal

When you decide to borrow money from the bank or the SBA, the first step you need to take is to write a loan proposal. This is not the same thing as a Business Plan, although some pieces of the proposal will look very similar.

There are also some similarites between your loan proposal and a grant proposal, particularly in the financial data. There are vast differences, however, between loans and grants. The grant is a cash award that need not be repaid in dollars. Sometimes the grant is paid back in the form of taxes, contributions to a healthy economy or benefits to the local community.

In contrast, a loan is money that must be repaid. It is a form of debt financing. A guaranteed loan, such as those made by the SBA, is a federal government guarantee to repay a private lender if the business defaults and fails to repay the loan.

Your "Sunday Best"

Think of the loan proposal as a portrait of your business that you are presenting to the lender. Like a special family photo, you'll want to dress up your business in its "Sunday best." The picture you show your lender may make the difference between getting a loan or being put on a long waiting list.

The bank will review your financial statements to analyze your company strengths and weaknesses. It will look for a well-organized proposal that shows you know what you're doing and that you will be a good "risk" for a loan.

Remember, bankers are not venture capitalists; they are not looking for innovative or exciting ideas. They want to know answers to these five questions:

1. How much money do you need to borrow?

2. For how long?

3. For what purpose?

4. When & how will you repay it?

5. What will you do if you don't get the loan?

The process of putting together your loan proposal, like developing your business plan, will help you focus on your goals and take an objective look at your business needs. See it as an opportunity to get your act together so you can get the money you need! Remember, the SBA loans over $7.4 BILLION DOLLARS a year to small businesses. All you have to do is take advantage of the information in this chapter, and soon, a piece of that pie could be going straight to you!

SBA Field Offices

The Field Offices of the Small Business Administration (SBA) have information available on SBA grants and loans. These offices are among the best sources of free information to assist you in starting up or expanding a small business. For more information call the SBA Hotline at 1-800-827-5722.

ALABAMA
2121 Eighth Avenue N, Suite 200
Birmingham, AL 35203-2398
Phone: (205) 731-1344
Fax: (205) 731-1404

ALASKA
222 W. Eighth Avenue, Room A36
Anchorage, AK 99513-7559
Phone: (907) 271-4022
Fax: (907) 271-4545

ARIZONA
2828 N. Central Avenue, Suite 800
Phoenix, AZ 85004-1093
Phone: (602) 640-2316
Fax: (602) 640-2360

ARKANSAS
2120 Riverfront Drive, Suite 100
Little Rock, AR 72202
Phone: (501) 324-5871
Fax: (501) 324-5199

CALIFORNIA
2719 N. Air Fresno Drive, Suite 107
Fresno, CA 93727-1547
Phone: (209) 487-5189
Fax: (209) 487-5292

330 N. Grand Blvd., Suite 1200
Glendale, CA 91203-2304
Phone: (818) 552-3210
Fax: (818) 552-3260

550 West C Street, Suite 550
San Diego, CA 92101
Phone: (619) 557-7252
Fax: (619) 557-5894

455 Market Street, 6th Floor
San Francisco, CA 94105-2420
Phone: (415) 744-6820
Fax: (415) 744-6812

200 W. Santa Ana Blvd., Suite 700
Santa Ana, CA 92701
Phone: (714) 550-7420
Fax: (714) 550-0191

COLORADO
721 19th Street, Room 426
Denver, CO 80202-2599
Phone: (303) 844-3984
Fax: (303) 844-6490

CONNECTICUT
Federal Bldg
330 Main Street, 2nd Floor
Hartford, CT 06106
Phone: (860) 240-4700
Fax: (86) 240-4659

DISTRICT OF COLUMBIA
1110 Vermont Avenue NW, Suite 900
Washington, DC 20036
Phone: (202) 606-4000
FLORIDA
1320 S. Dixie Hwy, Suite 301
Coral Gables, FL 33146-2911
Phone: (305) 536-5521
Fax: (305) 536-5058

7825 Bay Meadows Way, Suite 100-B
Jacksonville, FL 32256-7504
Phone: (904) 443-1900
Fax: (904) 443-1980

GEORGIA
1720 Peachtree Road NW, 6th Floor
Atlanta, GA 30309
Phone: (404) 347-4749
Fax: (404) 347-4745

HAWAII
300 Ala Moana, Room 2213
Honolulu, HI 96850-4981
Phone: (808) 541-2990
Fax: (808) 541-2976

IDAHO
1020 Main Street, Suite 290
Boise, ID 83702-5745
Phone: (208) 334-1696
Fax: (208) 334-9353

ILLINOIS
500 W. Madison Street, Room 1250
Chicago, IL 60661-2511
Phone: (312) 353-4528
Fax: (312) 886-5688

INDIANA
429 N. Pennsylvania Street, Suite 100
Indianapolis, IN 46204-1873
Phone: (317) 226-7272
Fax: (317) 226-7259

IOWA
215 Fourth Avenue SE, Suite 200
Cedar Rapids, IA 52402-1806
Phone: (319) 362-6405
Fax: (319) 362-7861

Room 749, New Federal Bldg.
210 Walnut Street
Des Moines, IA 50309
Phone: (515) 284-4422
Fax: (515) 284-4572

KANSAS
100 E. English Street, Suite 510
Wichita, KS 67202
Phone: (316) 269-6616

KENTUCKY
Room 188, Federal Building
600 Martin Luther King Place
Louisville, KY 40202
Phone: (502) 582-5971
Fax: (502) 582-5009

LOUISIANA
365 Canal Street, Suite 2250
New Orleans, LA 70130
Phone: (504) 589-6685
Fax: (504) 589-2339

MAINE
Room 512, Federal Bldg
40 Western Avenue
Augusta, ME 04330
Phone: (207) 622-8378
Fax: (207) 622-8277

MARYLAND
10 S. Howard Street, Suite 6220
Baltimore, MD 21201-2565
Phone: (410) 962-4392
Fax: (410) 962-1805

MASSACHUSETTS
10 Causeway Street, Room 265
Boston, MA 02222-1093
Phne: (617) 565-5590
Fax: (617) 565-5598

MICHIGAN
477 Michigan Avenue, Room 515
Detroit, MI 48226
Phone: (313) 226-6075
Fax: (313) 226-4769

MINNESOTA
100 North 6th Street, Suite 610-C
Minneapolis, MN 55403-1563
Phone: (612) 370-2324
Fax: (612) 370-2303

MISSISSIPPI
101 W. Capitol Street, Suite 400
Jackson, MS 39201
Phone: (601) 965-4378
Fax: (601) 965-4294

MISSOURI
323 W. Eighth Street, Suite 501
Kansas City, MO 64105
Phone: (816) 374-6708
Fax: (816) 374-6759

815 Olive Street, Room 242
St. Louis, MO 63101
Phone: (314) 539-6600
Fax: (314) 539-3785

MONTANA
301 S. Park Avenue, Room 334
Helena, MT 59626
Phone: (406) 441-1081
Fax: (406) 441-1090

NEBRASKA
11145 Mill Valley Road
Omaha, NE 68154
Phone: (402) 221-4691
Fax: (402) 221-3680

NEVADA
301 E. Steward Street, Room 301
Las Vegas, NV 89125-2527
Phone: (702) 388-6611
(Fax: (702) 388-6469

NEW HAMPSHIRE
143 N. Main Street, Room 202
Concord, NH 03301-1257
Phone: (603) 225-1400
Fax: (603) 225-1409

NEW JERSEY
2 Gateway Center, 4th Floor
Newark, NJ 07102
Phone: (201) 645-2434
Fax: (201) 645-2375

NEW MEXICO
625 Silver Street, Room 320
Albuquerque, MN 87102
Phone: (505) 766-1870
Fax: (505) 766-1057

NEW YORK
Room 1311, Federal Bldg.
111 W. Huron Street
Buffalo, NY 14202
Phone: (716) 551-4301
Fax: (716) 551-4418

26 Federal Plaza, Room 3100
New York, NY 10278
Phone: (212) 264-2454
Fax: (212) 264-4963

100 S. Clinton Street, Room 1073
Syracuse, NY 13260
Phone: (315) 448-0423
Fax: (315) 448-0402

NORTH CAROLINA
200 N. College Street, Suite A2015
Charlotte, NC 28202-2137
Phone: (704) 344-6563
Fax: (704) 344-6769

NORTH DAKOTA
Room 219, Federal Bldg.
657 Second Avenue N
Fargo, ND 58108-3086
Phone: (701) 239-5131
Fax: (701) 239-5645

OHIO
1111 Superior, Suite 630
Cleveland, OH 44144-2507
Phone: (216) 522-4180
Fax: (216) 522-2038

2 Nationwide Plaza
Columbus, OH 43215-2592
Phone: (614) 469-6860
Fax: (614) 469-2391

OKLAHOMA
210 Park Avenue, Suite 1300
Oklahoma City, OK 73102
Phone: (405) 231-5521
Fax: (405) 231-4876

OREGON
1515 SW Fifth Avenue, Suite 1050
Portland, OR 97201
Phone: (503) 326-2682
Fax: (503) 326-2808

PENNSYLVANIA
475 Allendale Road, Suite 201
King of Prussia, PA 19406
Phone: (610) 962-3800
Fax: (610) 962-3795

1000 Liberty Avenue, Room 1128
Pittsburgh, PA 15222
Phone: (412) 395-6560
Fax: (412) 395-6562

RHODE ISLAND
380 Westminister Street, 5th Floor
Providence, RI 02903
Phone: (401) 528-4561
Fax: (401) 528-4539

SOUTH CAROLINA
1835 Assembly Street, Room 358
Columbia, SC 29202
Phone: (803) 765-5377
Fax: (803) 765-5962

SOUTH DAKOTA
110 S. Phillips Avenue, Suite 200
Souix Falls, SD 57102-1109
Phone: (605) 330-4231
Fax: (605) 330-4215

TENNESSEE
50 Vantage Way, Suite 201
Nashville, TN 37228-1500
Phone: (615) 736-5881
Fax: (615) 736-7232

TEXAS
4300 Amon Cantor Blvd., Suite 114
Fort Worth, TX 76155
Phone: (817) 355-1933
Fax: (817) 885-6516

10737 Gateway West, Suite 320
El Paso, TX 79935
Phone: (915) 540-5676

222 E. Van Buren Street, Room 500
Harlingen, TX 78550
Phone: (956) 427-8533
Fax: (956) 427-8537

9301 SW Freeway, Suite 550
Houston, TX 77074-1591
Phone: (713) 773-6500
Fax: (713) 773-6550

1611 Tenth Avenue, Suite 200
Lubbock, TX 79401-2693
Phone: (806) 472-7462

727 E. Durango, 5th Floor
San Antonio, TX 78206
Phone: (512) 229-5900

UTAH
Room 2237, Federal Bldg.
125 S. State Street
Salt Lake City, UT 84138-1195
Phone: (801) 524-5804
Fax: (801) 524-4160

VERMONT
Room 205, Federal Bldg.
87 State Street
Montpelier, VT 05602
Phone: (802) 828-4422
Fax: (802) 828-4485

VIRGINIA
1504 Santa Rosa Road
Richmond, VA 23229
Phone: (804) 771-2400
Fax: (804) 771-8018

WASHINGTON
1200 Sixth Avenue, Suite 1700
Seattle, WA 98101
Phone: (206) 553-7310
Fax: (206) 553-7099

601 First Avenue W., 10th Floor E
Spokane, WA 99204-0317
Phone: (509) 353-2800

WEST VIRGINIA
168 W. Main Street, 5th Floor
Clarksburg, WV 26301
Phone: (304) 623-5631

WISCONSIN
212 E. Washington Avenue, Room 213
Madison, WI 53703
Phone: (608) 264-5261
Fax: (608) 264-5541

WYOMING
Room 4001 Federal Bodg.
100 East B Street
Caspar, WY 82602-2839
Phone: (307) 261-6500
Fax: (307) 261-6535

Business Information Centers

Business Information Centers (also known as BICs), are run by the SBA and are an incredible source of free information for you and your business. BICs have on-site libraries at your disposal. You can also explore the Information Age—you can learn about the latest computer equipment for your business, get help with market research through interactive videos and current databases, use the latest spreadsheet and planning software, and prepare graphic presentations. Most services are free of charge.

If your state does not have a Business Information Center listed here, call the SBA Hotline at 1-800-827-5722 and ask for the Center nearest you. Some states are planning to have an office open later this year.

ALABAMA
Alabama Business Information Center
No office at this time.

ALASKA
Alaska Business Information Center
No office at this time.

ARIZONA
Arizona Business Information Center
2828 N. Central Avenue, Suite 1800
Phoenix, AZ 85004
Phone: (602) 640-2316

Arkansas Business Information Center
100 S. Main Street, Suite 401
Little Rock, AK 72201
Phone: (501) 324-9043

CALIFORNIA
California Business Information Centers
U. S. Small Business Administration
3600 Wilshire Blvd., Suite L100
Los Angeles, CA 90010
Phone: (213) 251-7253
Fax: (213) 251-7255

U.S. Small Business Administration
San Diego District Office
550 West C Street, Suite 550
San Diego, CA 92101
Phone: (619) 557-7252
Fax: (619) 557-5894

Business Information Center
Southwestern College
900 Otay Lake Road, Suite 1601
Chula Vista, CA 91910
Phone: (619) 482-6375
Fax: (619) 482-6402

Business Information Center
455 Market Street, 6th floor
San Francisco, CA 94105-2420
Phone: (415) 744-6827
Fax: (415) 744-6812

COLORADO
Colorado Business Information Center
U.S. Small Business Administration
Denver District Office
721 19th Street, Suite 426
Denver, CO 80202-2599
Phone: (303) 844-3986
Fax: (303) 844-6490

CONNECTICUT
Connecticut Business Information
Center
Connecticut Small Business-Key to the
Future, Inc.
Hartford Civic Center
1 Civic Center Plaza, Suite 301
Hartford, CT
Phone: (860) 251-7000
Fax: (860) 251-7006

DELAWARE
Delaware Business Information Center
Delaware Small Business Resource &
Information Center
1318 N. Market Street
Wilmington, DE 19801
Phone: (302) 831-1555
Fax: (302) 831-1423

DISTRICT OF COLUMBIA
District of Columbia Business Informa-
tion Center
SBA/Bell Atlantic
Washington District Office
1110 Vermont Avenue N.W., Suite 900
Washington, DC 20043-4500
Phone: (202) 606-4000 x266
Fax: (202) 606-4225

FLORIDA
Florida Business Information Center
49 N.W. Fifth Street
Miami, FL 32128
Phone: (305) 374-1899
Fax: (305) 374-1882

GEORGIA
Georgia Business Information Center
U.S. Small Business Administration
Atlanta District Office
1720 Peachtree Road N.W., 6th floor
Atlanta, GA 30309
Phone: (404) 347-4749
Fax: (404) 347-2355

HAWAII
Hawaii Business Information Center
Bancorp
130 Merchant Street, Suite 1030
Honolulu, HI 96850-4981
Phone: (808) 522-8131
Fax: (808) 541-3650

IDAHO
Idaho Business Information Center
U.S. Small Business Administration
Boise District Office
1020 Main Street
Boise, ID 83702-5745
Phone: (208) 334-9077
Fax: (208) 334-9353

ILLINOIS
Illinois Business Information Center
U.S. Small Business Administration
Chicago District Office
500 W. Madison Street, Suite 1250
Chicago, IL 60661-2511
Phone: (312) 353-1825
Fax: (312) 886-5688

INDIANA
Indiana Business Information Center
Phone: (317) 226-7272

IOWA
Iowa Business Information Center
No office at this time.

KANSAS
Kansas Business Information Center
No office at this time.

KENTUCKY
Kentucky Business Information Center
No office at this time.

LOUISIANA
Louisiana Business Information Center
No office at this time.

MAINE
Maine Business Information Center
The Bates Mill Complex
35 Canal Street
Lewiston, ME 04240
Phone: (207) 622-8242
Fax: (207) 783-7745

MARYLAND
Maryland Business Information Center
SBA/NationsBank/MBDA/Bell Atlantic
Small Business Resource Center
3 W. Baltimore Street
Baltimore, MD 21201
Phone: (410) 605-0990
Fax: (410) 605-0995

MASSACHUSETTS
Massachusetts Business Information
Center
U.S. Small Business Administration
Boston District Office
10 Causeway Street, Room 265
Boston, MA 02222-1093
Phone: (617) 565-5615
Fax: (617) 565-5598

MICHIGAN
Michigan Business Information Center
No office at this time.

MINNESOTA
Minnesota Business Information Center
No office at this time.

MISSISSIPPI
Mississippi Business Information Center
No office at this time.

MISSOURI
Missouri Business Information Center
U.S. Small Business Administration
Kansas City District Office
323 West 8th Street, Suite 104,
Kansas City, MO 64105
Phone: (816) 374-6675
Fax: (816) 374-6692

Business Information Center
121 S. Meramec Avenue
Lobby Level
St. Louis, MO 63105
Phone: (314) 854-6861
Fax: (314) 889-7687

MONTANA
Montana Business Information Center
U.S. Small Business Administration
301 S. Park, Room 334
Helena, MT 59626
Phone: (406) 441-1081
Fax: (406) 441-1090

NEBRASKA
Nebraska Business Information Center
U.S. Small Business Administration
11141 Mill Valley Road
Omaha, NE 68154
Phone: (402) 221-3606
Fax: (402) 221-3680

NEVADA
Nevada Business Information Center
301 E. Stewart Avenue, Room 301
Las Vegas, NV 89101
Phone: (702) 388-6611
Fax: (702) 388-6469

NEW HAMPSHIRE
New Hampshire Business Information
Center
No office at this time.

NEW JERSEY
New Jersey Business Information Center
U.S. Small Business Administration
2 Gateway Center, 4th floor
Newark, NJ 07102
Phone: (201) 645-6049
Fax: (201) 645-6265

NEW MEXICO
New Mexico Business Information
Center
625 Silver SW, Suite 320
Albuquerque, NM 87102
Phone: (505) 272-7986
Fax: (505) 766-1057

NEW YORK
New York Business Information Center
The Capital Resource Center
1 Computer Drive South
Albany, NY 12205
Phone: (518) 446-1118 x31
Fax: (518) 446-1228

NORTH CAROLINA
North Carolina Business Information
Center
U.S. Small Business Administration
NationsBank/MBDA/Bell South
Small Business Resource Center
200N. College Street, Suite A2015
Charlotte, NC 28202-2137
Phone: (704) 344-9797
Fax: (704) 344-9990

NORTH DAKOTA
North Dakota Business Information
Center
No office at this time.

OHIO
Ohio Business Information Center
No office at this time.

OKLAHOMA
Oklahoma Business Information Center
U.S. Small Business Administration
UCO Small Business Development
Center
115 Park Avenue
Oklahoma City, OK 73102
Phone: (405) 232-2376
Fax: (405) 232-1967

OREGON
Oregon Business Information Center
SBA/Confederated Tribes of the Warm
Springs
Economic Development Office
2107 Wasco Street
Warm Springs, OR 97761
Phone: (503) 553-3592
Fax: (503) 553-3593

SBA/Confederated Tribes of the Ronde
Community
9615 Grand Ronde Road
Grande Ronde, OR 97347
Phone: (503) 879-2476
Fax: (503) 879-2479

BA/The Klamath Tribes
P.O. Box 436
Chiloquin, OR 97624
Phone: (541) 783-3402
Fax: (541) 783-2029

PENNSYLVANIA
Pennsylvania Business Information
Center
No office at this time.

RHODE ISLAND
Rhode Island Business Information
Center
U.S. Small Business Administration
380 West Minister Street, Room 511
Providence, RI 02903
Phone: (401) 528-4688
Fax: (401) 528-4539

Enterprise Community Center
550 Broad Street
Providence, RI 02907
Phone: (401) 272-1083
Fax: (401) 272-1186

SOUTH CAROLINA
South Carolina Business Information
Center
SBA/NationsBank/MBDA/Bell South/
College of Charleston
Small Business Resource Center
284 King Street
Charleston, SC 29401
Phone: (803) 853-3900
Fax: (803) 853-2529

SOUTH DAKOTA
South Dakota Business Information
Center
No office at this time.

TENNESSEE
Tennessee Business Information Center
SBA/NationsBank/MBDA
Small Business Resource Center
3401 West End Avenue
Nashville, TN 37203
Phone: (615) 749-4000
Fax: (615) 749-3685

TEXAS
Texas Business Information Center
SBA/Greater El Paso Chamber of
Commerce
10 Civic Center Plaza
El Paso, TX 79901
Phone: (915) 534-0531
Fax: (915) 534-0513

U.S. Small Business Administration
Ft. Worth Business Assistance Center
100 East 15th Street, Suite 400
Ft. Worth, TX 76102
Phone: (817) 871-6028
Fax: (817) 871-6031

U. S. Small Business Administration
Houston District Office
9301 Southwest Freeway, Suite 550
Houston, TX 77074-1591
Phone: (713) 845-2422
Fax: (713) 773-6550

U.S. General Store for Small Business
5400 Griggs Road
Houston, TX 77021
Phone: (713) 643-8000
Fax: (713) 643-8193

UTAH
Utah Business Information Center
169 East 100 South
Salt Lake City, UT 84111
Phone: (801) 364-1331
Fax: (801) 364-1310

VERMONT
Vermont Business Information Center
Vermont Technical College
Hartness Library
Randolph Center, VT 05061
Phone: (802) 828-4518
Fax: (802) 728-1506

VIRGINIA
Virginia Business Information Center
No office at this time.

WASHINGTON
Washington Business Information Center
U.S. Small Business Administration
Seattle District Office
1200 Sixth Avenue, Suite 1700
Seattle, WA 98101-1128
Phone: (206) 553-7311
Fax: (206) 889-0235

SBA/Spokane Chamber of Commerce
Business Information Center
1020 W. Riverside
Spokane, WA 99201
Phone: (509) 353-2800
Fax: (509) 353-2600

WEST VIRGINIA
West Virginia Business Information
Center
SBA/WVHTC Foundation
1000 Technology Drive
Fairmont, WV 26554
Phone: (304) 368-0023
Fax: (304) 367-2717

WISCONSIN
Wisconsin Business Information Center
No office at this time.

WYOMING
Wyoming Business Information Center
100 East B Street, Room 4001
Caspar, WY 82601
Phone: (307) 261-6500
Fax: (307) 261-6535

Chapter 11
Federal and State
Funding Sources

Federal Grant Programs

There are many ways you can find out about Federal Grant Programs for your business. Here are just a few: go to your local library and check out the U.S. Government Directory of Publications; read the business section of your local newspaper and the *Wall Street Journal*; join a trade association in your field; or read the latest on-line information relating to your business. Also, see Appendix D in *Free Cash Grants Vol. 2* for sources of Federal grants for businesses. Some of these sources are described in detail below.

Small Business Innovation Research

If you are in research, you'll want to look into the Small Business Innovation Research program (SBIR).This program came about due to Federal legislation passed in 1982. The purposes of the program are to stimulate research and development in technological innovation; to encourage participation by minorities and disadvantaged firms in R & D; and to allow small businesses to compete for federal funds.

SBIR money is available from federal agencies for Research & Development projects; about one-third of the awards go to companies with 10 or fewer employees. It is highly competitive, with most of the money coming from the Department of Defense. The program is coordinated by the SBA, although it is funded by the various government agencies listed below.

Each agency has different requirements for formal proposals and these are changed frequently, so you should contact them directly before you prepare or submit a funding proposal. Representatives in the Departments of Agriculture, Commerce, Defense, Education, Energy, Health & Human Services, Transportation, Environmental Protection Agency, NASA, the National Science Foundation, and the Nuclear Regulatory Agency can answer your questions about their agency SBIR programs & funding requirements.

Write or phone the agencies listed below to find out about their SBIR plans and financing requirements.

Department of Agriculture
SBIR/SBA Corrdinator
409 Third Street SW 8th Floor
Washington DC 20416
(202) 205-7777

Department of Defense
SBIR Program Manager
The Pentagon Rm 2A340
Washington DC 20301-3061
1-800-225-DTIC

Department of Energy
SBIR Program Mgr. ER-16
1000 Independence Ave SW
Washington DC 20585
(202) 586-5000

Environ. Protection Agency
Program Mgr. R & D/ SBIR
401 M Street SW, Mail Code 8722
Washington DC 20460
(202) 564-6838

National Science Foundation
SBIR Program Mgr.
Washington DC 20550
1-800-673-6188

Department of Education
SBIR Program Director
555 New Jersey Ave NW, 5th Floor
Washington DC 20208
(202) 219-2050

Department of Health & Human Services
Office of the Secretary/SBIR Progrm
200 Independence Ave SW Rm 513D
Washington DC 20201
(202) 690-7300

Department of Transportation
DOT SBIR Director
55 Broadway Kendall Square
Cambridge MA 02142-1093
(617) 494-2343

NASA
SBIR Office, NASA Hdqtrs.
300 E Street SW
Washington DC 20546-0001
(202) 358-0000

Nuclear Regulatory Agency
SBIR/SBA Representative
Washington DC 20555
(301) 415-7000

Insider's Tip:

Write to the SBA Office of Innovation Research & Technology, 409 Third Street SW, Washington, DC 20416, to receive a quarterly "Pre-solicitation Announcement" listing the agencies that will make SBIR offerings with the closing dates for applications. You can also get this information at your local public library in the Commerce Business Daily.

Writing an SBIR Proposal

A typical SBIR proposal will look much like the outline for a business plan described in Chapter 9. You should:

1. Describe your product or service and the proposal for funding

2. Identify your competitors and elements of your marketing plan

3. List management and business references

4. Include financial statements and income projections

Your proposal will be evaluated by a special panal of experts who will rate it according to guidelines established by that particular agency. You must show that your proposal has met the specifications and that you can perform as stated in your contract bid. You must also be financially able to wait to be paid until all the paperwork is completed. This can sometimes be several months after an award is made.

Farmer's Home Administration Business & Industrial Loans (FmHA)

This program guarantees up to 90% of loans made by commercial lenders to improve businesses located in rural communities (up to 50,000 population). The FmHA does not have as many restrictions as SBA loans. There are a number of different kinds of funding.

Money is available in areas that otherwise would not get commercial loans for business acquisition, publishing enterprises, or land purchase for farm or non-farm businesses. The program is administered through the Department of Agriculture. Loan approval is based solely on need and the planned uses for the money.

Loans are also available for youngsters aged 10-20 in rural towns to fund income-producing endeavors. Examples of this type of financing include money for equipment repair, landscaping, catering, craft production, raising livestock, or a number of other small business ventures.

For more information about these programs, write or call:

Farmer's Home Administration
Rural Business Cooperative Service
U.S. Department of Commerce
Washington, DC 20250
(202) 720-4323.

Other Federal Resources

• The U.S. Department of Commerce Federal Information Center is a wealth of information about patents, copyrights, federal assistance programs, grant sources and governement auctions. Call 1-800-688-9889.

• Another valuable resource available at any Government Depository Library (usually located in large cities and University libraries) is the Catalog of Federal Domestic Assistance (CFDA), a comprehensive listing of every program in every agency of the federal government. This Catalog is also available on the World Wide Web.

• The Government Printing Office has many publications for sale to help you get started in business. Contact the Superintendent of Documents, Government Printing Office, Washington DC 20402 (202) 512-1800. Here are some titles of interest if you want to know about government contracting with military and civil service agencies, or the sale of surplus property:

Small Business Subcontracting Directory

Women Business Owners: Selling to the Federal Government

U.S. Government Purchasing and Sales Directory

For general information about market trends, population, jobs, crime, vehicle registrations or other statistics, you need:

Statistical Abstract of the United States (available in hard cover or paperback).

The Proposal

You will need a PROPOSAL to submit to federal agencies for funding, just as you need a business plan to get money from private lenders through the SBA. First, follow the guidelines in the application packet exactly. Each agency has different specifications. In general, you need to submit the following:

- TITLE PAGE - Include the amount of money you are requesting, name of business (or agency), purpose and time frame of your project, your name, address, phone and fax numbers, and date of application.

- SUMMARY - Write a letter or brief paragraph describing your project. <u>Make it exciting to the reader as this may be the only section the agency will read before deciding to fund your project.</u>

- STATEMENT OF PURPOSE - Talk about your goals; what you will do and how you will do it. Include a timeline for completion of significant parts of the project.

- DESCRIPTION - Fully describe, in detail, the activities and who will participate. Include biographies of managers, advisors, and others who will assist you.

- FINANCIAL DATA - Budget, cash flow statement and other financial documents.

- EVALUATION METHOD - How will you know you have accomplished what you said you would do with the project.

- Most important, make sure your proposal is complete and that it answers every question in the application.

State and Local Business Resources

Each state has a variety of funding programs and assistance available for residents of that state. Some of these programs are geared to special needs for regional areas.

Many of the federally funded SBA programs listed above are administered by State agencies. In addition, there are Community Development Block Grants for rehabilitation of commercial buildings and creation of low- to- moderate- income job opportunities, and a number of other funding sources.These can include: matching grants, revenue or general obligation bonds, loans and loan guarantees, and interest subsidies. Interest subsidies are arrangements where the State will pay up to one-half the interest on your loan. They are particularly attractive for fledgling businesses.

Most states provide hotline numbers, Internet sites and free booklets on topics of interest to new business. Here's how to locate these FREE opportunities to grow your business!

Call Your State Congressional Office

One of the first places to look at the state level is your Congressional Office. Find the number in your phone directory and you can obtain information about agencies that have money available in your state, legislative changes that might affect your business, procurement data (how to sell to the government), surplus property sales, patent information, Veteran's Assistance programs, and a wealth of other information.

Like Federal grant programs, there are many specific programs available from sources within each state and at the local govenment level. These programs range from technical assistance and education (how to apply for assistance or write a grant proposal) to how to manage your company and sell your products or services. In 1995, for example, there was nearly $5 million available for growth and expansion of businesses in local communities located near National Forests.

Agencies at the State Level

• **Governor's Office** - In each state, agencies to assist business growth and development have advocacy resources in the Governor's office. Staff can help connect you with the appropriate source to meet your business needs. In many states, there is an Office of Minority and Women Owned Business which can assist in identifying contract opportunities and certifying your business for bidding on state and federal contracts. Other agencies may be Economic or Industrial Development, Import/Export Information or Financing, Office of Entrepreneurship, Department of Labor, or other related titles.

• **State Department of Trade and U.S. Department of Commerce District Office** - Obtain licensing and permit regulations; information about starting or expanding your business; foreign trade opportunities and job markets overseas; and referrals to other agencies that provide small business assistance.

- **State Chamber of Commerce** - Many handbooks and other resources; start-up kits for new business; seminars and workshops; help in understanding state regulations and legislation affecting different kinds of business.

- **Small Business Development Centers** - There are more than 900 small business centers throughout the country to assist you with free advice on financial planning and technical aspects of owning and operating a small business. Each state has a lead organization responsible for setting up networks of satellite offices. Many of these centers are affiliated with local colleges and universities or coordinated through banks, chambers of commerce, or other local organizations. All are under the direction of the SBA. Funding is shared with states, colleges, foundations and corporations. In addition to one-on-one counseling, these centers provide complete resource libraries with on-line market and financial data bases. <u>See the list of Small Business Development Centers at the end of this chapter.</u>

Resources At The Local Level

- **Mayor's Office/Planning Departments** - The Mayor's staff can point you in the right direction for current changes in local restrictions and regulations on business operations; the planning offices have current zoning, parking and transportation regulations. Both provide you with valuable information about business trends in your community.

- **Local Chamber of Commerce** - This is a great way to network with local business people who meet regularly to provide assistance and create support for small business within the community. Chamber committees provide demographics and economic information, labor and market trends, current changes in local laws, and related workshops to help you make planning decisions for your business. Many local corporations provide experts and mentors to help new businesses in the community.

- **Financial Institutions** - Your local banker can help you get started or assist you in solving problems that arise in your business; get acquainted as soon as you can, and you may find a valuable source of funding in an emergency or a good reference when you need to borrow for expansion.

• **Business incubators** - Also known as innovation, enterprise, or technology centers; these are programs, often located near universities or colleges, that provide a number of services for fledgling businesses; services range from low rent office or warehouse spaces to meeting rooms, secretarial support, financial assistance, training and other support services.

• **Local education institutions** - Many Community colleges have classes for entrepreneurs which provide training in management, planning, employee relations, budget and finance, and other business skills. They also hold seminars andworkshops open to the public, and often support business centers that offer introductory services as well as advanced training in a variety of business fields.

• **Public Library** - A wealth of reference materials are available here; you can learn 'how-to' for almost any aspect of your business.

Small Business Development Centers

There are more than 900 Small Business Development Centers throughout the country to assist you with free advice on financial planning and technical aspects of owning and operating a small business. These centers are under the direction of the SBA. Some of them are listed below. For more information call the SBA Hotline at 1-800-872-5722.

Alabama
Alabama SBDC Consortium
University of Alabama at Birmingham
Medical Towers Building
1717 Eleventh Avenue, Suite 419
Birmingham, AL 35294-4410
Phone: (205) 934-7260
Fax: (205) 934-7645

Alaska
Alaska Small Business Development Center
University of Alaska Anchorage
430 W. Seventh Avenue, Suite 110
Anchorage, AK 99501
Phone: (907) 274-7232
Fax: (907) 274-9524

Arizona
Arizona SBDC Network
2411 West 14th Street, Suite 132
Tempe, AZ 85281
Phone: (602) 731-8720
Fax: (602) 731-8729

Arkansas
Arkansas Small Business Development
University of Arkansas at Little Rock
100 S. Main, Suite 401
Little Rock, AR 72201
Phone: (501) 324-9043
Fax: (501) 324-9049

California
California SBDC Program
Department of Commerce
801 K Street, Suite 1700
 Sacramento, CA 95814
Phone: (916) 322-3502
Fax: (916) 322-5084

Colorado
Colorado Small Business Development
Center
Colorado Office of Business Develop-
ment
1625 Broadway, Suite 1710
Denver, CO 80202
Phone: (303) 892-3809
Fax: (303) 892-3848

Connecticut Small Business Develop-
ment Center
University of Connecticut
2 Bourn Place MTS, U-94
Storrs, CT 06269-5094
Phone: (860) 486-4135
Fax: (860) 486-1576

Delaware
Delaware Small Business Development
Center
University of Delaware
MBNA Building, Room 102
Newark, DE 19716-2711
Phone: (302) 831-2747
Fax: (302) 831-1423

District of Columbia
District of Columbia SBDC
Howard University
2600 Sixth Street, Room 128
Washington, DC 20059
Phone: (202) 806 1550
Fax: (202) 806 1777

Florida
Florida Small Business Development
Center Network
University of West Florida
19 W. Garden Street, Suite 300
Pensacola, FL 32501
Phone: (904) 444-2060
Fax: (904) 444-2070

Georgia
Georgia Small Business Development
Center
University of Georgia
Chicopee Complex
1180 E. Broad Street
Athens, GA 30602-5412
Phone: (706) 542-7436
Fax: (706) 542-6776

Hawaii
Hawaii Small Business Development
Center Network
University of Hawaii at Hilo
200 W. Kiwili
Hilo, HI 96720
Phone: (808) 974-7515
Fax: (808) 974-7683

Idaho
Idaho Small Business Development
Center
Boise State University
1910 University Drive
Boise, ID 83725
Phone: (208) 385-1640
Fax: (208) 385-3877

Illinois
Illinois Small Business Development
Center
Department of Commerce & Commu-
nity Affairs
620 E. Adams Street, 3rd floor
Springfield, IL 62701
Phone: (217) 524-5856
Fax: (217) 785-6328

Indiana
Indiana Small Business Development
Centers
One N, Capitol, Suite 420
Indianapolis, IN 46204
Phone: (317) 264-6871
Fax: (317) 264-3102

Iowa
Iowa Small Business Development
Center
Iowa State University
137 Lynn Avenue
Ames, IA 50014
Phone: (515) 292-6351
Fax: (515) 292-0020

Kansas
Kansas Small Business Development
Center
Wichita State University
1845 Fairmont
Wichita, KS 67260-0148
Phone: (316) 978-3193
Fax: (316) 978-3647

Kentucky
Kentucky Small Business Development
Center
University of Kentucky, Center for
Business Development
225 Business and Economics Building
Lexington, KY 40506-0034
Phone: (606) 257-7668
Fax: (606) 323-1907

Louisiana
Louisiana Small Business Development
Center
Northeast Louisiana University, CBA
700 University Avenue
Monroe, LA 71209-5506
Phone: (318) 342-5506
Fax: (318) 342-5510

Maine
Maine Small Business Development
Center
University of Southern Maine
P.O. Box 9300
96 Falmouth Street
Portland, ME 04104-9300
Phone: (207) 780-4949
Fax: (207) 780-4810

Maryland Small Business Development
Center Network
Dept. of Economic and Employment
Development
7100 Baltimore Ave., Ste. 405
College Park, MD 20740-3627
Phone: (301) 403-8300
Fax: (301) 403-8303

Massachusetts
Massachusetts Small Business Develop-
ment Center
University of Massachusetts
School of Management, Room 205
Amherst, MA 01003
Phone: (413) 545-6301
Fax: (413) 545-1273

Michigan
Michigan Small Business Development
Center
Wayne State University
2727 Second Avenue, Suite 107
Detroit, MI 48201
Phone: (313) 964-1798
Fax: (313) 964-3648

Minnesota
Minnesota Small Business Development
Center
500 Metro Square
121 Seventh Place East
St. Paul, MN 55101-2146
Phone: (612) 297-5770
Fax: (612) 296-1290

Mississippi
Mississippi Small Business Development
Center
University of Mississippi
Old Chemistry Building, Suite 216
University, MS 38677
Phone: (601) 232-5001
Fax: (601) 232-5650

Missouri
Missouri Small Business Development
Center
University of Missouri
1205 University Ave., Ste. 300
Columbia, MO 65211
Phone: (573) 882-0344
Fax: (573) 884-4297

Montana
Montana Small Business Development
Center
Department of Commerce
1424 Ninth Avenue
Helena, MT 59620
Phone: (406) 444-4780
Fax: (406) 444-1872

Nebraska
Nebraska Small Business Development
Center
University of Nebraska at Omaha
60th & Dodge Street, CBA Room 407
Omaha, NE 68182
Phone: (402) 554-2521
Fax: (402) 554-3747

Nevada
Nevada Small Business Development
Center
University of Nevada in Reno
College of Business Administration-032,
Room 411
Reno, NV 89557-0100
Phone: (702) 784-1717
Fax: (702) 784-4337

New Hampshire
New Hampshire Small Business Devel-
opment Center
University of New Hampshire
108 McConnell Hall
Durham, NH 03824
Phone: (603) 862-2200
Fax: (603) 862-4876

New Jersey
New Jersey Small Business Develop-
ment Center
Rutgers University
Graduate School of Management
49 Bleeker Street
Newark, NJ 07102-1993
Phone: (973) 353-5950
Fax: (973) 353-1030

New Mexico
New Mexico Small Business Develop-
ment Center
6401 Richards Avenue
Santa Fe, NM 87505
Phone: (505) 438-1362
Fax: (505) 471-9469

New York
New York Small Business Development
Center
State University of New York
State University Plaza S-523
Albany, NY 12246
Phone: (518) 443-5398
Fax: (518) 465-4992

North Carolina
North Carolina Small Business Develop-
ment Center
8701 Mallard Creek Road
Charlotte, NC 28262
Phone: (704) 548-1090
Fax: (704) 548-9050

North Dakota
North Dakota Small Business Develop-
ment Center
University of North Dakota
118 Gamble Hall, Box 7308
Grand Forks, ND 58202
Phone: (701) 777-3700
Fax: (701) 777-3225

Ohio
Ohio Small Business Development
Center
77 S. High Street
P.O. Box 1001
Columbus, OH 43266-0101
Phone: (614) 466-2711
Fax: (614) 466-0829

Oklahoma
Oklahoma Small Business Development
Center
S.E. Oklahoma State University
P.O. Box 2584, Station A
Durant, OK 74701
Phone: (405) 924-0277
Fax: (405) 920-7471

Oregon
Oregon Small Business Development
Center
Lane Community College
44 W. Broadway, Suite 501
Eugene, OR 97401-3021
Phone: (541) 726-2250
Fax: (541) 345-6006

Pennsylvania
Pennsylvania Small Business Develop-
ment Center
The Wharton School
Vance Hall, 4th floor
3733 Spruce Street
Philadelphia, PA 19104-6374
Phone: (215) 898-1219
Fax: (215) 573-2135

Rhode Island
Rhode Island Small Business Develop-
ment Center
Bryant College
1150 Douglas Pike
Smithfield, RI 02917
Phone: (401) 232-6111
Fax: (401) 232-6933

South Carolina
The Frank L. Roddey Small Business
Development Center
University of South Carolina
College of Business Administration
Columbia, SC 29208
Phone: (803) 777-4907
Fax: (803) 777-4403

South Dakota
South Dakota Small Business Develop-
ment Center
University of South Dakota
414 E. Clark
Vermillion, SD 57069
Phone: (605) 677-5279
Fax: (605) 677-5272

Tennessee
Tennessee Small Business Development
Center
University of Memphis
Building 1, South Campus
Memphis, TN 38152
Phone: (901) 678-2500
Fax: (901) 678-4072

Texas
North Texas Dallas Small Business
Development Center
Bill J. Priest Institute for Economic
Development
1402 Corinth Street
Dallas, TX 75215
Phone: (214) 860-5850
Fax: (214) 860-5881

University of Houston Small Business
Development Center
1100 Louisiana, Suite 500
Houston, TX 77002
Phone: (713) 752-8444
Fax: (713) 756-1500

N.W. Texas Small Business Development
Center
Texas Tech University
2579 S. Loop 289, Suite 114
Lubbock, TX 79423
Phone: (806) 745-3973
Fax: (806) 745-6207

UTSA South Texas Border Small Business
Development Center
UTSA Downtown Center
1222 N. Main Street, Suite 410
San Antonio, TX 78212
Phone: (210) 458-2450
Fax: (210) 458-2464

Utah
Utah Small Business Development
Center
Salt Lake Community College
8811 S. 700 East
Sandy, UT 84070
Phone: (801) 255-5991
Fax: (801) 255-6393

Vermont
Vermont Small Business Development
Center
Vermont Technical College
P.O. Box 422
Randolph, VT 05060
Phone: (802) 728-9101
Fax: (802) 728-3026

Virginia
Virginia Small Business Development
Center
P.O. Box 798
901 E. Byrd Street
Richmond, VA 23218-0798
Phone: (804) 371-8253
Fax: (804) 225-3384

Washington
Washington Small Business Develop-
ment Center
Washington State University
501 Johnson Tower
Pullman, WA 99164-4851
Phone: (509) 335-1576
Fax: (509) 335-0949

West Virginia
West Virginia Small Business Develop-
ment Center
950 Kanauwha Blvd. East
Charleston, WV 25301
Phone: (304) 558-2960
Fax: (304) 558-0127

Wisconsin
Wisconsin Small Business Development Center
University of Wisconsin
432 N. Lake Street, Room 423
Madison WI 53706
Phone: (608) 263-7794
Fax: (608) 263-7830

Wyoming
Wyoming Small Business Development Center
State Network Office
P.O. Box 3922
Laramine, WY 82071-3275
Phone: (307) 766-3505
Fax: (307) 766-3406

Chapter 12
Venture Capital Sources

Another potential source of funding for some new business enter prises is private venture capital. Venture capital, sometimes called risk capital, is money provided by professional investers to help a company get started. There are nearly 1,000 such firms in the U.S. (including the SBICs regulated by the SBA and local banks). This money is usually offered in exchange for future profits or a percentage of ownership in the company.

Venture capitalists assume a huge risk by taking a chance on an unproved business venture. They expect a sizable return (usually 5 to 10 times) on their investment money. Usually venture capital is best suited for high tech ventures rather than retail stores or service businesses.

Think B-I-G

If you have a great idea or vision and can think B-I-G, a venture capitalist may be the right source of funding for your business. That's because most venture capitalists don't want to bother with small loans. They are looking for companies with big potential, and they are willing to take big risks (i.e., million-dollar investments) for a piece of the action.

That piece could be nearly half your company, so be careful! You may have heard horror stories of companies swallowed up by the "venture capital sharks." Such cases do exist, but usually the venture capitalists just want to be sure they'll make money on the deal. Most of the time they want a 'hands-on' opportunity to see that you do the job right.

You will also need to think before you talk when you're shopping for a venture capital firm. Some states have regulations about the number of people you can talk to about your new business venture without violating securities laws.

How to Excite a Venture Capitalist

A venture capitalist will get excited about your business if you can offer the following:

- A history of succcess in this or other endeavors; strong management skills

- The potential for "going public" (selling stock in your corporation)

- Significant others in the deal (strong partners or supporters)

- Potential for permanence (will it be there tomorrow?)

- Vision for the future

Insider's Tip:

Equity investors are gambling on your idea in the hope that you can make them rich. If you give up 40-60% of your company and it is highly successful, you later may regret it! Be especially careful when you negotiate terms with a venture capitalist.

Banks vs. Venture Capitalists

There are a number of differences between what a bank, or lender, is seeking and what a venture capitalist wants. Here are a few of those differences:

Venture Capitalist	Lender (bank)
Looks for high profile company with quick growth potential; visible risk/reward ratio	Looks for low-risk; stability
Looks for high profit potential	Looks for slow, but consistent growth and profit
Looks for ownership opportunity;	Looks for sound management
Will take over company, if necessary to meet objective	Not interested in managing or taking over a company if owner defaults on loan
Looks for new ideas, innovation	Looks for proven track record

Your Venture Capital Proposal

Just as you need a grant proposal or a loan package for other types of financing, you need to submit a business plan for venture capital. The best way to accomplish this is to put together a team of advisors. The most important member of that team will be your controller, or VP of Finance, because venture capital proposals are especially heavy on financial reports and projections. You'll also need some legal and accounting advice and an advertising or marketing consultant.

How To Find Venture Capital

Your first step in raising venture capital is to research possible sources and select the best prospects for your particular business proposal. You can begin by contacting one of the agencies listed below for a directory of their members. Then call one or two and find out what they are seeking.

Above all, don't waste your time talking to the wrong people. Make sure you have found a suitable match before you submit your business plan.

Remember, venture capital is an equity (ownership) source of funding, NOT a debt (loan). For this reason, be sure that you are willing to give up part of your company (often 25%-70%) in exchange for some start-up money.

National Venture Capital Association (NVCA)

The National Venture Capital Association (NVCA) started as a nonprofit organization in the early 1970's. It is a professional group of financiers and private venture capitalists. A directory listing addresses and phone numbers of more than 200 members is available for $40 by mailing your request with check or money order payable to NVCA to:

The National Venture Capital Association (NVCA)
1655 North Fort Meyer Drive, Suite 700
Arlington VA 22209
(703) 351-5269
FAX (703) 351-5268

Venture Capital Clubs

Throughout the country, there are Venture Capital Clubs whose members help each other in finding sources for money and advice for new business ventures. In Southern California, for example, there is an organization called the Orange County Venture Network that meets monthly on the UC Irvine Campus. It is a nonprofit group with a mission to assist, educate, and connect early start-up growth companies. They publish a directory of members and sponsor workshops and forums throughout the year.

See Appendix H in *Free Cash Grants Vol. 2* for a list of additional venture capital resources.

Insider's Tip:

Go to your public library and take a look at Stanley Pratt's *Guide to Venture Capital Sources*. Most libraries will have it in the reference department.

What About Private Investors?

Maybe you have a great business idea that doesn't fit the requirements for standard loans or grants. Where can you turn for help? Try a private placement. You can exchange a percentage of ownership in your company for money (without going public with sale of stock) by making a private offering to no more than 25 people. This is a limited partnership, usually with friends, acquaintances and/or their friends who are willing to make a small investment in your company.

HOWEVER, if you want to use this source of funding, you're going to need some professional advice—specifically, an attorney and an experienced stockbroker to help you prepare the legal documents required for a private placement. This type of funding is generally works best for larger companies that are trying to raise money for a new product. Most private placements are highly speculative. But if your have a business with a track record and new product development is your thing, a private placement may be right for you.

Chapter 13
Make Your Business
A Winner!

Common-Sense Tips for Successful Entrepreneuring

• Many would-be entrepreneurs skip one of the most important steps in building a successful business - market research. While large companies spend hundreds of thousands of dollars on surveys and studies to preview the market and discover what people will buy, small business owners often "wing it." Don't make that mistake. An SBA or SCORE advisor can help you survey the market in your area.

• A second problem for new entrepreneurs is pricing their goods and services. For the product, you need to add material cost (everything needed to make the product), direct labor (cost of workers benefits & wages), overhead (insurance, rent, utilities, advertising, etc.), and a markup (usually 20-35%). A service business includes all of the above, but just phrased in a different way that represents an hourly fee. Be sure your price is competitive within your market area. <u>Set your fees and product prices carefully so that your business can remain profitable.</u>

• Instead of buying ads in the local paper, learn how to create a story and get free publicity for your business. Take a class in publicity or get a SCORE advisor to help you.

• Need a temporary office for a meeting or conference overseas? The American Embassy can help with space, translation, printing and other services. Call the International Trade Information Centers of the U.S. Department of Commerce, 1-800-USA-TRADE.

• Need a home inspection to be sure your work space is safe? Call the National Institute for Occupational Safety and Health at 1-800-356-4674.

• Need some counseling to help you get started? Use the resources available at the local, state, and federal level to make your business successful. Call SBA for a list of SCORE volunteers in your area. 1-800-827-5722.

• Don't try to fool Uncle Sam. Be straight with the I.R.S. For tax questions (filing Schedule C for small business, what you can and cannot deduct, depreciation schedules to use, etc.) Call the IRS at 1-800-424-1040 or 1-800-4243676; or you can write:

> Tax Services, Irs
> U.S. Dept. of the Treasury
> 1111 Constitution Ave. NW
> Washington, DC 20224

A list of basic publications, free of charge from the I.R.S. includes:

Pub. 334	Tax Guide for Small Business
Pub. 463	Travel, Entertainment, & Gift Expense
Pub. 533	Self-Employment Tax
Pub. 534	Depreciation
Pub. 535	Business Expenses
Pub. 583	Recordkeeping for Small Business
Pub. 587	Business Use of Your Home

• Join an Association, such as the National Federation of Independent Business (NFIB, 1-615-872-5800) or the National Association for the Self -Employed (NASE, 1-800-232-NASE). They can provide additional advocacy, business assistance, and networking opportunities as you grow your enterprise.

• Demonstrate that YOU are serious about building your business for the long term. Be frugal. Think cheap! When you are getting started, it is tempting to buy a few "trappings" to impress people. DON'T. Most people (and particularly potential lenders or investors in your business) will be much more impressed by your ability to spend wisely and budget carefully.

• If you are a Woman Business Owner or want to know more about services, trends, or projections for women in business, Call (202) 219-6666 or write:

> Women's Bureau
> U.S. Department of Labor
> 200 Constitution Ave. NW
> Washington DC 20210

• Call the Federal Information Center for an expert on nearly any topic: 1-301-722-9000 or write:

> Federal Information Center
> P.O. Box 600
> Cumberland MD 21501-0600

• Once you've completed your business plan, regardless how elaborate or simple it may be, it is worthless unless you use it. Start today!

Final Checklist For New Enterpreneurs

1. Decide what kind of business you want to start.

2. Research the market.

3. Contact your local SCORE volunteers.

4. Set your goals and objectives.

5. Write a Business Plan.

6. Seek funding (if needed).

7. GO FOR IT!

If you are truly excited about going into business, you will rise to the challenge. Keep the faith. Visualize your success. Then work to make it happen!

Chapter 14
Free Cash Grants
For Health Care

Every year billions of dollars in grants are awarded to Americans in need of health care and social services. This money come from Federal and State governments, private and corporate foundations, and private nonprofit associations. The United States Census Bureau estimates that in 1995, $25 billion was given away to U.S. residents by State and Federal governments for medical purposes. In addition to this, private and corporate foundations granted $13 billion to individuals. That's a total of $38 billion available each year for medical care.

$38 billion!! This money is given in addition to the $187 billion Medicare and Medicaid annual expenditures allotted by the Federal government; and in addition to the $100 billion spent by State governments on health care such as MediCal. And on top of that there are many organizations that give away FREE social services, FREE psychotherapy, FREE vacations for entire families, FREE prescriptions, and FREE hospital care.

One of the largest categories of grants to individuals is grants for general welfare and medical assistance—that is, free cash for emergency or long-term personal, medical, or living expenses. Another large category of grants is grants-in-aid—which means that instead of money, you get free equipment or services that can help you when you're ill—everything from free wheelchairs to seeing eye dogs. Thankfully, the funding agencies that make these awards have made it easy to apply for them. Most of the foundations you will be applying to require just a few basic pieces of information. See the checklist in this chapter for details.

In the following chapters, we'll show you how to find the right source of medical assistance, how to apply, and what to expect. We'll also give you the details on free medical grants and services throughout the nation available to you and your family members. They include:

Self-Help Groups — organizations that can lead you to important medical information and sources of financial assistance.

Veteran's Benefits — special assistance for Veterans, their spouses and dependents.

Viatical Associations — insurance buy-outs for the terminally ill.

Service Organizations — providers of gifts and services, such as The Make-A-Wish Foundation; Wellness Centers; support groups; and other non-profit organizations that exist to help individuals suffering from nearly every disease.

Foundations — private organizations that make grants to individuals with medical needs.

In *Free Cash Grants Volume 2*, you'll find a detailed list of grant sources for medical needs arranged by state. Remember, no matter what you need, there's a wealth of resources waiting to be claimed—and they're yours just for the asking!

Getting the Grant You Need

You've heard the old saying, "Anything worth doing is worth doing right." When it comes to getting free cash grants, even grants you clearly deserve, it makes all the difference to follow the few basic steps we've outlined below. Remember, you're not the only person out there seeking free cash grants! You want your application to stand out in the crowd. Following the steps below will do just that and improve your chances of receiving the money and services you need.

Know Your Condition

In order to get the help you need, you must first know what is wrong with you so that you can accurately describe yourself and your condition to the grantmakers. That may sound obvious, yet many people applying for grants do not give a clear description of their situation, either medically or financially. Ask yourself the following questions. (If you are seeking grants for a relative or friend, then ask them the same questions.)

• What is the nature of my condition?

• What is the technical term for my illness?

• How long have I been in treatment?

• Is my condition temporary, chronic or terminal?

• What is the <u>prognosis</u>? (That is, what is my doctor's <u>prediction of the outcome</u> of my illness or condition?)

• What is my current financial status?

• What are my current assets? (Stocks, insurance policies, real estate, etc.)

Know Your Needs

Take a few steps back from yourself and honestly evaluate your present situation. Then ask yourself two very important questions, writing down the answers:

• How could my life be improved right now? (For instance, Do I need money to pay my medical bills?)

• What do I genuinely need in order to continue living without deprivation?

Pick the Right Grants

To shop for a grant, first look over the listings in *Free Cash Grants, Volume 2*, to see which ones fit your situation. For instance, if you have a child with a life-threatening illness, look for everything that has to do with children and diseases in the listings. You should also look for listings that apply to the particular disease. Using this method can introduce you many types of awards that you had no idea about.

We know of one family with a gravely ill child who discovered The Hole-in-the-Wall Gang summer camp. It wasn't until they read about this free camp that they realized their child could benefit by being in a loving, fun atmosphere for two weeks away from the hospital visits and the often stressful life at home.

Insider's Tip:

Look over the listings in Volume II VERY CAREFULLY to determine which grants are most appropriate for your needs. Most rejections of grant requests happen for the simple reason that the applicant is asking the wrong foundation, charity, or government source. Pay close attention to the restrictions and qualifications for each grant, and eliminate the ones least likely to assist you.

The Initial Contact

Your next step is to contact each potential grant source by mail or phone to verify all current information:

• Check their address, telephone, name of the proper contact person, and his or her title.

• If there is no contact name, begin your letter, "To Whom It May Concern."

• Whether you make your initial inquiry by mail or phone, ask for a copy of the source's <u>most current assistance guidelines</u>, and an <u>application form</u> if one is required.

• Ask about <u>application deadlines</u>.

• Ask <u>where they are in the funding cycle</u>. For instance, if there is no deadline, when is the best time for you to apply? For example, many foundations schedule their board of directors meetings in advance for the year. An informed applicant will submit an application well ahead of the board meeting.

• Ask <u>when the awards will be announced</u>.

• Ask <u>when the funds will be distributed</u>.

• Whenever you are speaking with a foundation or granting source, remember to be on your best behavior. <u>Always be prepared to talk about why you are applying and what you are applying for.</u>

Preparing Your Application

The first impression your application makes goes a long way towards getting the grant you need. Grantmakers want to know you took the time and trouble to fill out the application correctly. Make sure that you answer all the questions on the application, and follow all the instructions exactly.

Filling out your first application can be a time-consuming process. However, once you've finished one, you can use your write-up about your personal history and the details of your condition on many other grant applications.

Sometimes granting committees require a personal essay giving your "statement of purpose." Don't be put off if the granting source requires an essay. Get your ideas down on paper and then ask a friend, preferably a good writer, to critique it for you. Take your time to rewrite when necessary.

Be prepared to submit tax returns and other financial records. You should know that in most cases you will not be penalized for having money in the bank or for owning your own home.

Finally, develop a list of personal references. Be sure to get strong references from people who know you well and think you're an honorable person. Call all of the people whose names you plan to use, and ask their permission to be included with your application.

The Appeal Letter

Not all grantmakers have an application form for you to fill out. In these cases, the way to present yourself in the best possible light is by writing a simple, straightforward letter from the heart. This kind of honest appeal will take you far, and will cause the decision-makers to pay attention.

Above all, remember to be clear, concise and neat! To write a good letter requires a clean, white piece of paper, a business-size envelope, a typewriter, and most important, a clear, focused outline of who you are and what your specific needs are. This is how you will let the granting source know <u>why</u> they should award <u>you</u> their money or their services.

Insider's Tip
Apply to a number of funding sources for grants and awards, as no one application is guaranteed to win an award. Remember, the more sources you apply to, the greater your chances for success!

Summary Checklist For a Successful Grant Application

1. <u>A brief, concise letter</u> outlining your medical problem and/or expenses and bills you have incurred because of this problem. In the final paragraph of your letter you should specify a dollar amount that you feel confident would ease your financial burden. For instance:

"I request a grant in the amount of $3,000 to help pay the costs associated with a visiting nurse, which is not covered by my medical insurance."

<u>Remember to pay special attention to the maximum award given by the foundation to which you are applying</u>. If the foundation only gives grants up to $15,000 and you need $20,000, you can only request $15,000 from that foundation.

2. <u>A report from the doctors or hospital staff</u> involved with your care.

3. <u>A copy of your tax return</u>. Don't worry! You will not be penalized for showing excellent earnings or for having savings. The most important issue is how your medical costs will alter your financial stability.

4. <u>A personal interview</u>. This interview may take place by phone or in person. Be prepared to simply state the facts of your case and needs, and all will go well.

5. <u>Follow up</u>. Mark your calendar with the date you mailed your application. Write the name of the foundation/association, and then mark the date on which the awards are due to be announced. Wait one day from the announcement date, and then call the foundation to learn whether or not you received your requested grant.

If you were not granted the aid you need from one foundation, simply go on to the next. When pursuing grants, always try to contact at least four foundations/associations in any three-month period. There are two reasons for this. A single grant source may not be able to give enough money cover your needs, and your chances of receiving aid improve the more grants you apply for.

We know that any kind of rejection can be discouraging—especially for a grant that you really want. So if your request is rejected, see if you can find out why through a polite request to the foundation. Knowing the reason will help you apply more successfully in the future.

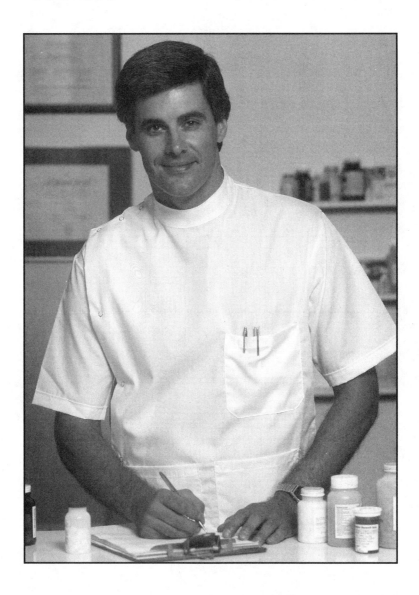

Chapter 15
Self-Help Groups

There are over 750 national self-help groups for medical conditions in the United States. No matter what illness or condition you or a family member may be suffering from, you can find free information and aid through organizations that exist to help individuals with specific medical conditions.

These groups deal with nearly every disease or concern you can imagine. This chapter has a complete list of the hundreds of diseases, disorders, conditions, and life situations for which you can find self-help groups.

While self-help groups do not offer free cash grants, they can provide you with valuable information and lead you to sources of financial help, grants-in-aid, and other free services. Most groups have a monthly or bi-monthly newsletter which lists sources of aid, plus updates on the latest medical developments regarding your condition. That's why it pays to check out self-help groups as soon as possible when you're faced with an illness or any other challenging life situation.

The Magic of Self-Help Clearinghouses

The easiest way to find out about self-help groups is through self-help clearinghouses. There are two national organizations that can be of special help. First, the American Self-Help Clearinghouse provides leads and information to individuals seeking a specific self-help group. They will also provide you with information on any state or local self-help clearinghouse that serves your area. These state and local clearinghouses can tell you about local groups that may not be part of a national self-help organization. You can even learn how to start your own self-help group.

For a free listing of phone contacts for self-help clearinghouses in the United States, call or send a stamped self-addressed envelope with your request to:

American Self-Help Clearinghouse
c/o Northwest Covenant Medical Center
25 Pocono Road
Denville, New Jersey 07834-2995
(973) 625-9565

The second national organization that can help you find self-help groups is the National Self-Help Clearinghouse. For information and referrals to self-help groups and regional self-help clearinghouses write or call:

National Self-Help Clearinghouse
c/o CUNY, Graduate School and University Center
25 West 43rd Street, Room 620
New York, New York 10036
(212) 354-8525

Finally, see the listings by state at the end of this chapter to get you started. With all the help available out there, you're sure to find a self-help group that can make a difference in your life!

Help is available for people facing the following illnesses, disorders, and life situations:

18q. Chromosome Deficiency
49XXXXY Syndrome
8-P Duplication
Aarskog Syndrome
Accident Victims
Achromatopsia
Acid Maltase Deficiency
Acidemia
Addison's Disease
Adrenal Disease
Agenesis of the Corpus Callosum
Agoraphobia
Aicardi Syndrome
AIDS
Alagille Syndrome
Albinism
Alcohol Abuse
Allergy
Alopecia Areata
ALS
Alstrom's Syndrome
Alzheimer's Disease
Amputation
Androgen Insensitivity
Anemia
Anencephaly
Angelman Syndrome
Ankylosing Spondylitis
Anophthalmia
Anorchidism
Anxiety Attacks
Apert Syndrome
Apnea, sleep
Arachnoiditis
Arnold-Chiari Malformation
Arthritis
Arthrogryposis
Asperger Syndrome
Ataxia
Attention Deficit Disorder
Autism
Autoimmune Disorders
Batten's Disease
Beckwith-Wiedemann
Behcet's Syndrome
Bell's Palsy
Benign Essential Blepharospasm
Bi-Polar

Blepharophimosis Ptosis Epicanthus Inversus
Blind
Blood Disease
Bone Marrow Transplant
Brachial Plexus Injury
Brain Tumor
Breast Cancer
Burn Survivors
Campus Groups
Cancer
Carbohydrate Deficient Glycoprotein
Carcinoid
Carnitine Deficiency
Carpal Tunnel Syndrome
Celiac Sprue
Cerebral Palsy
Cesarean Birth
CFC Syndrome
Charcot-Marie-Tooth
CHARGE Syndrome
Chemical Hypersensitivity
Cholecystectomy Injury
Chromosome Disorders
Chronic Illness
Chronic Fatigue Syndrome
Cleft Palate
Claca
Cobalamin
Cockayne Syndrome
Codependency
Coffin-Lowry Syndrome
Cohen Syndrome
Coma
Congenital Adrenal Hyperplasia
Congenital Central Hypoventilation
Congential Cytomegalovirus Disease
Congenital Hypothyroidism
Convulsive Disorders
Cornelia De Lange
Cortico-Basal Ganglionic Degeneration
Costello Syndrome
Creutzfeldt-Jakob Disease
Cri du Chat (5P) Syndrome

Cystic Hygroma
Cystinosis
Cystinuria
Cytochrome C Oxidase Deficiency
Dandy Walker Syndrome
Deaf
Delayed Sleep Phase Syndrome
Depression
Desmoid Tumor
Diabetes Insipidus
Diabetes
DiGeorge Syndrome
Donors' offspring
Down Syndrome
DPT Vaccine Injury
Drug Abuse
Dysautonomia
Dysfunctional Families
Dystonia
Ear Anomalies
Eating Disorders
Ectodermal Dysplasias
Ectopic Pregnancy
Ehlers Danlos Syndrome
Emotional Abuse
Emphysema
Encephalitis
Environmental Illness
Eosinophilia-Myalgia Syndrome
Epilepsy
Erb's Palsy
Extracorporeal Membrane Oxygenation
Facial Disfigurement
Facioscapulohumeral Muscular Dystrophy
Fam Erythronphagotic Lymphohistiocytosis
Families of Mentally Ill
Fatty Oxidation Disorder
Fetal Loss
Fetal Alcohol Syndrome
Fibrodysplasia Ossificans Progressiva
Fibromyalgia
Fragile X Syndrome
Freeman-Sheldon
Gastroesophageal Reflux

Gastroplasty
Gaucher Disease
Genetic Disorders
Glycogen Storage Disease
Granulomatous Disease, Chronic
Graves Disease
Guillain-Barre Syndrome
Head Injury
Headaches
Hearing Impaired
Heart
HELLP Syndrome
Hemanigioma
Hemifacial Spasm
Hemimegalencephaly
Hepatitis
Hereditary Hemorrhagic
  Telangiectasia
Hermansky-Pudlak Syndrome
Hernia, Congenital Diaphragmatic
Herpes
High Risk Infants
Hirschsprung's Disease
Histiocytosis-X
Human Papilloma Virus
Huntington's Disease
Hydrocephalus
Hyperacusis
Hyperhidrosis
Hyperlexia
Hypoglycemia
Hypoparathyroidism
Hypophosphatasia
Hypospadias
Hypotonia
Idiopathic Thrombocytosis
Ill Children
Immune Disorders
Impotency
Incontinence
Incontinentia Pigmenti
Infertility
Inflammatory Bowel Disease
Interstitial Cystitis
Intestinal Multiple Polyposis
Intraventricular Hemorrhage
Inverted Duplication 15
Irritable Bowel Syndrome
Ivemark Syndrome
Joseph Disease
Joubert Syndrome
Kidney Disease

Klinefelter Syndrome
Klippel Feil Syndrome
Klippel-Trenaunay
Lactic Acidosis
Landau-Kleffner Syndrome
Laparoscopic Injury
Laryngectomy
Latex Allergy
Laurence Moon Bardet Biedl
  Syndrome
Lead Poisoning
Learning Disability
Lesch-Nyhan Disease
Leukodystrophy
Life Threatening Illness
Lightning Victims
Limb Deficiency
Lissencephaly
Liver Disease
Lou Gehrig's Disease
Lowe Syndrome
Lupron Drug Use
Lupus
Lyme Disease
Lymphangioleiomyomatosis
Lymphedema
Lymphocytosis
Malignant Hyperthermia
Malpractice
Manic-Depression
Marfan Syndrome
Mastocytosis
McCune-Albright Syndrome
Meniere's Disease
Menke's Disease
Mental Retardation
Metabolic Disorders
Metatropic Dysplasia Dwarfism
Microphthalmia
Miller's Syndrome
Miscarriage
Missing persons
Mitochondrial Disorders
Moebius Syndrome
Monosomy Disorders
Mood Disorders
Mucolipidosis Type 4
Mucopolysaccharidoses
Multiple Endocrine Neoplasm Type 1
Multiple Hereditary Exostoses (MHE)
Multiple Sclerosis
Multiple Symmetrical Lipomatosis

Multiple Myeloma
Muscular Dystrophpy
Myalgic Encephalomyelitis
Myasthenia Gravis
Myelin Disorders
Myeloprolifeative Disease
Myoclonus
Myositis
Myotubular Myopathy
Nager Syndrome
Narcolepsy
Nemaline Myopathy, Congenital
Neurofibromatosis
Neurometabolic Disorder
Neutropenia
Nevoid Basal Cell Carcinoma
Nevus, Congenital
Niemann Pick Type C
Noonan Syndrome
Obsessive-Compulsive Disorder
Ollier's Disease
Opitz Syndrome
Opsoclonus-Myoclonus Syndrome
Osteogenesis Imperfecta
Osteoporosis
Ostomy
Overweight
Oxalosis & Hyperoxaluria
Paget's Disease
Pain, Chronic
Pallister-Killian
Papillomatosis Juvenile
  Laryngotracheal
Parkinsons's Disease
Peripheral Nerve Disease
Phenylketonuria
Phobias
Physical Abuse
Physical Disabilities (General)
Pituitary Disorders
Polio
Pompe Disease
Porphyria
Post-Partum Depression
Potter Syndrome
Prader-Willi Syndrome
Progressive Osseous Heteroplasia
Progressive Supranuclear Palsy
Prostate Problems
Prozac
Pseudo-obstruction
Pseudotumor Cerebri

Pseudoxanthoma Elasticum
Radiation
Rare Disorders, General
Raynaud's Disease
Reflex Anoxic Seizure Disorder
Reflex Sympathetic Dstrophy
Respiratory Disease
Restless Leg Syndrome
Retinoblastoma
Rett Syndrome
Reye's Syndrome
Robinow Syndrome
Rubinstein-Taybi Syndrome
Russell-Silver Syndrome
Sarcoidosis
Scleroderma
Scoliosis
Shock Victims
Shprintzen Syndrome
Shwachman Syndrome
Shy-Drager Syndrome
Sjogren's Syndrome
Skin Disease
Smith-Lemli-Opitz
Smith-Magenis Syndrome
Soto Syndrome
Spasmodic Dysphonia
Spasmodic Torticollis
Spina Bifida
Spinal Muscular Atrophy
Step Cell Transplant
Stickler Syndrome
Strep, Group B
Stroke
Sturge-Weber
Stuttering
Suicide Survivors
Surgical Injury
Syringomyelia
Takayasu's ArteritisTall
Taste Disorder
Tay-Sachs Disease
Temporomandibular Joint
   Dysfunction (TMJ)
Thrombocytopenia Absent Radius
Thrombotic Thrombocytoponic
   Purpura
Thyroid Problems
Tic Douloureux
Tinnitus
Tourette Syndrome
Tracheo Esophageal Fistula

Transplant Recipient, Organ
Transverse Myelitis
Trauma
Treacher Collins Syndrome
Trigeminal Neuralgia
Trisomy
Tube-Feeding
Tuberous Scierosis
Turner's Syndrome
Type One Fiber Hypotrophy
Urea Cycle Disorders
Vascular Malformations
Vestibular DisordersVeterans
Visually impaired
Von Hippel Lindau
Weaver Syndrome
Wegener's Granulomatosis
William's Syndrome
Wilson's Disease
Wolf-Hirschhorn Syndrome
Xeroderma Pigmentosum

NATIONAL

American Self-Help Clearinghouse

Maintains database of national self-help headquarters and model one-of-a-kind groups. Referrals to self-help clearinghouses nationwide. Offers assistance to persons interested in starting new groups. Publishes directory of national support groups; newsletter. Write: American Self-Help Clearinghouse, c/o Northwest Covenant Med. Ctr., 25 Pocono Rd., Denville, NJ 07834. Call (973) 625-9565; FAX: (973) 625-8848: TTD: (973) 625-9053, E-mail: ashc@cybernex.net Website: http://www.cmhc.com/selfhelp.

National Self-Help Clearinghouse

Provides information and referral to self-help groups and regional self-help clearinghouses. Encourages and conducts training of professionals about self-help. Carries out research activities. Publishes manuals, training materials and a newsletter. Write: National Self-Help Clearinghouse, c/o CUNY, Graduate School and University Ctr., 25 W. 43rd St., Rm. 620, New York, NY 10036. Call (212) 354-8525; FAX: (212) 642-1956.

ALABAMA

SHINE

Volunteer-run self-help clearinghouse that provides information on self-help groups in Birmingham area. Write: c/o Bill Russell, P.O. Box 7767, Birmingham, AL 35228. Call (205) 251-5912. Leave a message on answering machine and a volunteer will get back with you.

ARIZONA

Self-Help Umbrella

Information and referrals to support groups statewide. Assistance in starting groups. Write: Self-Help Umbrella, P.O. Box 472, Scottsdale, AZ 85252. Call (602) 231-0868.

ARKANSAS

Helpline

Information and referrals to self-help groups in the seven northeast counties. Literature on starting groups. Write: Helpline, P.O. Box 9028, Jonesboro, AR 72403-9028. Call (870) 932-5555; FAX (870) 931-5056; E-mail: janie@inso/wwb.net.

CALIFORNIA

Mental Health Association of Yolo County

Provides information and referrals to self-help groups in Yolo County. Offers assistance in starting local support groups. Training workshops, how-to materials, directory of local groups. Consultation to existing groups, conferences, speakers bureau. Write: MHA of Yolo County, P.O. Box 447, Davis, CA 95617. Call (916) 756-8181 (M-F, 9am-3pm).

SHARE

Provides information and referrals to self-help groups in the Los Angeles area. Technical assistance for new and ongoing self-help group meetings. Provides meeting space for groups. Write: SHARE!, 5521 Grosvenor Blvd., Los Angeles, CA 90066. Call (310) 305-8878 (Mon.-Fri, 10am-4pm PT; 24 hour voice mail with information on the most requested groups).

Mental Health Association

Provides training and technical assistance to people starting new groups. Collects data on existing groups and identifies the need for new groups. Conducts community education about self-help. Write: MHA, 8912 Volunteer Lane, Ste. 130, Sacramento, CA 95826-3221. Call (916) 368-3100; FAX: (916) 368-3104.

Self-Help Connection

Provides information and referrals to free and low cost mental health support groups in San Diego County. Also provides support in starting and maintaining support groups. Publishes yearly directory of groups. Write: Self-Help Connection, c/o MHA San Diego County, 2047 El Cajon Blvd., San Diego, CA 92104-1091. Call (619) 543-0412.

Helpline

Information and referrals to support groups in 11 county areas. Provides assistance in starting groups and community educations. Also provides information and referrals to local services and agencies. Write: Helpline, N. Calif. Council for the Community, 50 California St., #200, San Francisco, CA 94111. Call 800-273-6222 (from 510,707 and 916 area codes) or (415) 772-4357; FAX (415) 391-8302; TTY: (415) 772-4440. (Mon-Fri, 8am-5pm). Accepts collect calls.

CONNECTICUT

Connecticut Self-Help Support Network

Information and referrals to support groups. Provides technical assistance in starting and maintaining groups, group leadership training, educational workshops and conferences. Publishes directory of self-help groups, newsletter, other publications. Write: c/o Terry Freeman, Consultation Center, 389 Whitney Ave., New Haven, CT 06511. Call (203) 624-6982; FAX (203) 562-6355.

HAWAII

United Self-Help

Dedicated to serving consumers of mental health services. Information and referrals to a variety of mental health self-help groups throughout Hawaii. Newsletter. Write: United Self-Help, 277 Ohua Ave., Honolulu, HI 96815. Call (808) 926-0466.

ILLINOIS

Illinois Self-Help Coalition

Provides assistance in starting groups, training workshops, consultation to existing groups, how-to materials, conferences, speakers bureau, directory of support groups. Write: Illinois Self-Help Coalition, Wright College, 3400 North Austin, Chicago, IL 60634. Call (773) 481-8837 (Mon., Thur., Fri., 9:30-4); FAX: (773) 481-8917; E-mail: dipeace@aol.com Website: http://www.selfhelp-illinois.org

Self-Help Center

Information and referrals to support groups. Directory and technical assistance in developing groups. Write: c/o MHA, 188 W. Randolph, #2225, Chicago, IL 60601. Call (312) 368-9070 (Mon-Fri, 9am-5pm).

Self-Help Center

Information and referrals to local support groups. Provides assistance in starting support groups, how-to materials, training workshops, directory, specialized group listings, newsletter, consultation to existing groups, and library of self-help literature. Write: Self-Help Center, Family Service, 405 S. State St., Champaign, IL 61820-5196. Call (217) 352-0099; FAX: (217) 352-9512; TDD: (217) 352-0160; Website: http://www.prairienet.org/selfhelp/

Macon County Support Group Network

Information and referrals to local support groups. Write: c/o Macon County Health Dept., 1221 E. Condit, Decatur, IL 62521. Call (217) 429-HELP (Mon-Fri, 9am-5pm).

KANSAS

Self-Help Network of Kansas

Provides information and referrals to self-help groups. Offers developmental assistance and consultation to existing groups or persons interested in starting groups. Provides community education, training workshops and conferences on self-help. Publishes directory of groups and conducts research. Write: Self-Help Network of Kansas, Wichita State University, Box 34, 1845 Fairmount, Wichita, KS 67260-0034. Call 800-445-0116 or (316) 978-3843; FAX (316) 978-3593. E-mail shnofks@wsuhub.uc.twsu.edu

MASSACHUSETTS

Massachusetts Clearinghouse of Mutual Help Groups

Provides information and referrals to support groups. Also provides consultation to persons interested in starting groups, and to groups already in existence. Publishes directory of self-help groups statewide. Write: c/o Massachusetts Cooperative Extension System, Dept. of Consumer Studies, 113 Skinner Hall, Univ. of Mass., Amherst, MA 01003. Call (413) 545-2313 or (413) 545-5013; FAX (413) 545-4410.

MICHIGAN

Michigan Self-Help Clearinghouse

Provides information and referrals to support groups statewide. Helps persons to start new groups. Provides consultation to existing groups. Provides "seeker" list to be connected to others who share same concerns. Research library, newsletter, speakers bureau, training workshops, written materials, and statewide directory. Write: Michigan Self-Help Clearinghouse, 106 W. Allegan, Ste. 300, Lansing, MI 48933-1706. Call (517) 484-7373 or 800-777-5556; FAX: (517) 487-0827.

Center For Self-Help

Information and referrals to support groups. Networks individuals, groups, professionals and agencies. Provides community education. Assists new groups, facilitates group meetings, and holds training workshops. Directory, newsletter. Write: Center for Help, Riverwood Center, Attn: Pat Friend, P.O. Box 547, Benton Harbor, MI 49023-0547. Call 800-336-0341 or (616) 925-0952. E-mail pfriend95@aol.com

MISSOURI

Mental Health Association of the Heartland

Provides information and referrals to local mental health services (support groups, agencies, mental health centers, community services). Provides public awareness and education. Speakers bureau, conferences, advocacy for mental health consumers, senior programs, and educational workshops for self-help group leaders. Directory of self-help groups. Write: MHA of the Heartland, 7611 State Line Rd., #230, Kansas City, MO 64114. Call (816) 822-7272; FAX: (816) 822-2388.

St. Louis Self-Help Clearinghouse

Provides information and referrals to all types of support groups in the St. Louis area. Helps interested persons to start support groups. Provides consultation and technical assistance to new and existing groups. Directory available. Write: St. Louis Self-Help Clearinghouse, c/o MHA of Greater St. Louis, 1905 S. Grand, St. Louis, MO 63104. Call (314) 773-1399; FAX: (314) 773-5930.

NEBRASKA

Nebraska Self-Help Information Services

Provides information and referrals to support groups. Offers assistance to new and existing groups. Acts as an answering service to groups. Presentations can be arranged for schools and other interested organizations. State Directory of self-help groups. Write: Nebraska Self-Help Info. Svcs., 1601 Euclid Ave., Lincoln, NE 68502. Call (402) 476-9668; FAX: (402) 434-3972; Website: http://incolor.inetnebr.com/jmfritts/selfhelp/

NEW JERSEY

New Jersey Self-Help Clearinghouse

Information on local to support groups. Assistance to new and existing groups. Workshops, conferences, directory of support groups. Write: NJSHC, c/o Northwest Covenant Medical Center, 25 Pocono Rd., Denville, NJ 07834. Call (973) 625-9565; FAX: (973) 625-8848; TDD: (973) 625-9053; E-mail: njsch@.cybernex.net

NEW YORK

New York City Self Help Center

Information and referrals to support groups in the five boroughs (Manhattan, Bronx, Staten Island, Queens, and Brooklyn). Assistance to new and developing groups. Write: NYC Self-Help Center, 120 W. 57th St., New York, NY 10019. Call (212) 586-5770; FAX: (212) 956-1652.

Brooklyn Self-Help Clearinghouse

Provides information and referrals to self-help groups in Brooklyn. Also offers consultation services. Support groups for mid-life women are a special focus of the Clearinghouse. Write: Brooklyn Self-Help Clearinghouse, 30 Third Avd., Brooklyn, NY 11217. Call (718) 875-1420.

Long Island Self-Help Clearinghouse

Provides referrals to local support groups. Assistance to new and existing groups. Write: Long Island Self-Help Clearinghouse, c/o NY College of Osteopathic Medicine, NY Institute of Technology, P.O. Box 8000, Old Westbury, NY 11568. Call (516) 626-1721 or 888-SELF-HLP; FAX: (516) 626-9290; E-mail: egiannetti@acl.nyit.edu

Westchester Self-Help Clearinghouse

A central resource for mutual support groups. Provides confidential information and referrals to groups. Assists in the formation of new groups. Trains mutual support group leaders, sponsors workshops and conference, and provides community education. Directory of self-help groups. Phone networks for newly widowed men and women, and newly separated women. Write: Westchester Self-Help Clearinghouse, 456 North St., White Plains, NY 10605. Call (914) 949-0788 ext. 237 voice mail; FAX: (914) 948-3783.

Self-Help Resource Center

Information and referrals to local self-help groups. Maintains an updated database and publishes a directory of local self-help groups. Works with established and prospective self-help group leaders to assist them in creating and/or developing their groups. Collaborates with community organizations and professionals to identify the need for new groups and to assist in organizing them. Write: Self-Help Resource Center, c/o MHA, 82 Oak St., Binghamton, NY 13905. Call (607) 771-8888; FAX: (607) 771-8892; e-mail: mhaofst@spectra.net

Self-Help Clearinghouse of Cattaraugus County

Provides information and referrals to local support groups in Cattaraugus and Alleghany counties. Offers assistance in starting new groups. Publishes self-help directory. Holds workshops for group leaders, helps groups find meeting places, and provides other technical assistance and referrals. Write: Self-Help Clearinghouse of Cattaraugus County, c/o American Red Cross, Greater Buffalo Chapter, P.O. Box 67, Olean, NY 14760. Call (716) 372-5800.

Information Line of United Way
Maintains a database of information on self-help support groups in the community. This information is also available in publication form that is updated on a yearly basis. The Information Line of United Way maintains and refers people to other services in the community. Write: Information Line of United Way, P.O. Box 832, Poughkeepsie, NY 12602. Call (914) 473-1500.

Erie County Self-Help Clearinghouse
Information and referrals to local self-help groups. Assistance to existing groups that meet at the Mental Health Association. Write: Erie County Self-Help Clearinghouse, c/o MHA of Erie County, Inc., 999 Delaware Ave., Buffalo, NY 14209. Call (716) 886-1242; FAX: (716) 881-6428.

HealthLink
Provides information and referrals to local self-help resources. Also publishes a directory of area support groups, and provides technical assistance to new and existing groups. Makes referrals to other local services and agencies. Write: HealthLink, Pyramid Mall, 246 N. Comrie Ave., Johnstown, NY 12095. Call (518) 736-1120.

Clearinghouse for Self-Help Groups
Provides information and referrals to local support groups. Assistance in starting new groups, training workshops, how-to materials. Consultation to existing groups, directory of local groups. Write: Clearinghouse for Self-Help Groups, 339 East Ave., Ste. 201, Rochester, NY 14604. Call Cindy LaCotta (716) 325-3145; FAX: (716) 325-3188.

Wellness Institute
Provides information and referrals about health education programs and support groups to persons throughout Montgomery County and surrounding areas. Write: Sr. Rita Jean Du Brey, Wellness Institute, St. Mary's Hospital, 427 Guy Park Ave., Amsterdam, NY 12010. Call (518) 842-1900, ext. 286.

Niagara Self-Help Clearinghouse
Information and referrals to local support groups. Provides technical assistance to new groups, and networks with other community resources. Helps new group development and holds group leader training. Newsletter, directory of self-help groups, mental health video/book library. Write: Niagara Self-Help Clearinghouse, c/o MHA of Niagara County, 151 East Avenue, Lockport, NY 14094. Call (716) 433-3780.

The Volunteer Center of the Mohawk Valley
Provides information and referrals to local support groups. Assistance to new and existing groups. Write: The Volunteer Center of the Mohawk Valley, 401 Columbia St., Utica, NY 13502. Call (315) 735-4463.

Helpline/Rapeline
Information and referrals to local support groups, 24-hour crisis intervention, information and referral to local services and agencies. Rape hotline. Directory of local services. Write: Helpline, MHA in Orange County, 20 John St., Goshen, NY 10924. Call 800-832-1200 or (914) 294-7411.

The Self-Help Clearinghouse
Information and referrals concerning self-help groups. Provides consultation and technical assistance to ongoing groups and to new groups that are forming. Publishes newsletter, self-help calendar, and directory of groups. Write: Self-Help Clearinghouse, c/o MHA of Rockland, 20 Squadron Blvd., New City, NY 10956. Call (914) 639-7400 Ext. 22; FAX: (914) 639-7419.

Mechanicville Area Community Services Center, Inc.
Information and referrals to local self-help groups. Provides consultation and technical assistance to existing groups. Write: Mechanicville Area Comm. Svcs. Ctr., Inc., P.O. Box 3, 6 South Main St., Mechanicville, NY 12118. Call (518) 664-8322; FAX: (518) 664-9457.

Reachout of St. Lawrence County
Provides information and referrals to local support groups and other services and agencies in St. Lawrence County. Also has information on national organizations. Provides limited consultation to existing and new groups. Acts as Alcoholics Anonymous answering service. Provides crisis intervention. Write: Reachout, P.O. Box 5051, Potsdam, NY 13676-5051. Call (315) 265-2422; FAX: (315) 265-1752; E-mail: reachout@slic.com

Institute for Human Services/HELPLINE
Information and referrals to local services and agencies, as well as support groups. Provides assistance to new and existing self-help groups. Also acts as 24-hour crisis line. Newsletter, information and referral, self-help clearinghouse. Write: Institute for Human Svcs., 29 Denison Pkwy. East, Ste. B, Corning, NY 14830. Call 800-346-2211; (607) 936-4114 (helpline).

HELPLINE Information and Referral Service

Provides information on area self-help groups. Also refers callers to other local services and agencies. Publishes a self-help group directory, a directory of resources of Syracuse and Onondaga Counties, and a Human Services Directory. Write: HELPLINE, The Volunteer Center, Inc., 115 E. Jefferson St., Ste. #400, Syracuse, NY 13202. Call (315) 474-7011.

Mental Health Association in Tompkins County

Provides information and referral, education, advocacy, respite and family support concerning mental health issues and services. Referrals to support groups and therapists. Publishes a support group guide, a guide to alternative therapists, a directory of local psychotherapists and a newletter. Write: MHA in Tompkins County, 225 S. Fulton St., Ste B, Ithaca, NY 14850. Call (607) 273-9250.

Mental Health Assocation in Ulster County

Information and referrals to local support groups. Assistance in starting mental health support groups, training workshops, how-to materials, consultation to existing groups. Offers directory, speakers bureau, training programs for families of the mentally ill, provides models for transitional groups. Write: MHA in Ulster County, P.O. Box 2304, Kingston, NY 12402-2304. Call (914) 339-9090, ext. 113.

Wyoming County Chapter American Red Cross

Provides information on local support groups and other services or agencies. Write: c/o Dale Palesh, Wyoming County Chapter American Red Cross, 25 W. Buffalo St., Warsaw, NY 14569. Call (716) 786-0540.

NORTH CAROLINA

SupportWorks Self-Help Clearinghouse

Provides information and referrals to support groups in Mecklenberg County. Networks persons seeking mutual support. Consultation to people developing new groups. Free or low cost telephone conference calls available to non-profit organizations. Outreach to underserved communities. Publication, "Power Tools" on starting groups. Write: SupportWorks, 1018 East Blvd., #5, Charlotte, NC 28203-5779. Call (704) 331-9500; FAX: (704) 332-2127.

NORTH DAKOTA

Hot Line

Information and referrals to support groups in the Fargo-Moorhead area. Directory of local support groups. Limited consultation to new and existing groups. Information and referrals to other local services and agencies. Write: Hot Line, P.O. Box 447, Fargo, ND 58107-0447. Call (701) 235-SEEK.

OHIO

Greater Dayton Self-Help Clearinghouse

Information and referrals to self-help groups in the Dayton area. Technical assistance provided to start new self-help groups. Group effectiveness workshops. Self-help group newspaper columns. Write: Great Dayton Self-Help Clearinghouse, c/o Family Service Assn., 184 Salem Ave., Dayton, OH 45406. Call (937) 225-3004; FAX: (937) 222-3710, TDD: (937) 222-7921.

The Greater Toledo Self-Help Network

Provides information and referrals to local self-help groups. Assists area professionals in locating groups for their clients. Provides consultation to new and existing groups, training workshops, and how-to guidelines. Write: c/o Harbor Behavioral Health Care, 4334 Secor Rd., Toledo, OH 43623. Call (419) 475-4449; FAX: (419) 479-3832.

OREGON

Northwest Regional Self-Help Clearinghouse

Maintains an extensive database of resources and self-help groups in Mulnomah, Clackamas and Washington Counties in Oregon, and Clark County in Washington. Assistance to new groups. Publishes Resource File, Self-Help Group Directory, and Human Services Directory. Write: Northwest Regional Self-Help Clearinghouse, Metro Crisis Intervention, P.O. Box 637, Portland, OR 97207. Call (503) 222-5555; FAX: (503) 499-4301.

PENNSYLVANIA

Valley Wide Help

Provides information on local support groups in the Lehigh Valley area. Also provides referrals to other agencies and services. Write: ValleyWide Help, c/o American Red Cross, 2200 Avenue A, Bethlehem, PA 18017-2181. Call (610) 865-4400; FAX: (610) 865-5871; TDD: (610) 866-0131.

Self-Help Group Network of the Pittsburgh Area

Maintains a listing of self help groups in the southwestern Pennsylvania. Provides referral services, information to those who would like to start new groups, consultation, seminars and resource materials on self-help. Publishes directory of self-help groups, newsletter. Write: Self Help Group Network of the Pittsburg Area, 1323 Forbes Ave., Ste. #200, Pittsburgh, PA 15219. Call (412) 261-5363; FAX: (412) 471-2722.

SHINE

Provides information and referrals to support groups in the Lackawanna County and northeastern Pennsylvania. Sponsors workshops and special events for self-help advocates. Brochure. Community resource library. Write: SHINE, 538 Spruce St., Ste 420, Scranton, PA 18503. Call (717) 961-1234; FAX: (717) 348-5816; E-mail: echase@maressa.com

SOUTH CAROLINA

Midlands Area Support Group Network

Provides information and referrals to self-help groups in Richland/Lexington County. Write: Midlands Area Support Group Network, c/o Lexington Medical Center, 2720 Sunset Blvd., W. Columbia, SC 29169. Call (803) 791-2800.

TENNESSEE

Mental Health Association of Greater Knoxville

Information and referrals regarding self-help groups in Knox County and surrounding areas. Consultation for persons interested in starting new groups and training for self-help group leaders. Publishes directory of local support groups, Speakers Bureau. Write: c/o Mental Health Assn. of Greater Knoxville, 110 Westfield Rd., #3, Knoxville, TN 37919. Call (423) 584-9125; E-mail: mha@korrnet.org; Website: http://www.korrnet.org/mha

Self-Help Clearinghouse

Information and referrals to local support groups. Public educational information forums on issues of mental health, professional training and seminars. Assistance in starting new groups, training workshops, directory of local groups, and consultation to existing groups, facilitator training, how-to guidelines. Speakers bureau. Write: Self-Help Clearinghouse, MHA of the Mid-South, 2400 Poplar Ave., #410, Memphis, TN 38112. Call (901) 323-8485; FAX: (901) 323-0858.

TEXAS

Texas Self-Help Clearinghouse

Provides information and referral to groups and agencies statewide and consultation to persons interested in starting new groups. Publishes technical manual for starting support groups; FAIR Facilitators Manual; and other manuals. Write: Texas Self-Help Clearinghouse, c/o MHA, 8401 Shoal Creek Blvd., Austin, TX 78757. Call (512) 454-3706; FAX: (512) 454-3725.

Dallas Self-Help Clearinghouse

Information and referrals to self-help groups. Printed information available for a small fee to those wishing to start groups. Write: Dallas Self-Help Clearinghouse, c/o MHA of Great Dallas, 2929 Carlisle, #350, Dallas, TX 75204. Call (214) 871-2420; FAX: (214) 954-0611.

Support Group Clearinghouse

Promotes self-help groups by collecting and disseminating information on local groups, educates the public about the benefits of self-help groups, and provides technical assistance to new and existing groups. Write: c/o Women's Resource Center, 1155 Idaho, Ste B, El Paso, TX 79902. Call (915) 544-0782; FAX: (915) 544-3913; E-mail: as796.rgfn.epcc.edu; Website: http://rgfn.epcc.edu/users/as796

UTAH

Information and Referral Center

Provides directory of self help groups in the Salt Lake City area. Also provides referral services and information on appropriate agencies and organizations. Write: 1025 S. 700 West, Salt Lake City, UT 84104 (801) 978-3333.

Chapter 16
Veteran's Health Benefits –
For Vets, Their Spouses &
Families

"To care for him who shall have borne the battle,

and for his widow and his orphan."

—Abraham Lincoln

More than 100 years ago, Abraham Lincoln declared that any American who served the United States as a member of the military should be granted special benefits. Today the Department of Veterans Affairs (VA) is one area where President Lincoln's vision is being served. This is good news to millions of U.S. residents, since more than one-third of America's population has ties to the armed services. This includes 23 million wartime veterans, 5 million peacetime veterans, 3 million active duty military personnel, and tens of millions of their dependents —spouses, children, and parents.

The VA provides a wide variety of loans and grants for veterans and their dependents—not the least of which are medical benefits and medical grants-in-aid. In addition, many state governments have programs that complement federal benefits. And on top of that, voluntary and other private organizations like the American Legion have raised millions of dollars to provide financial aid to their members, other veterans and military personnel, and their dependents.

How can you find out what benefits are available for you? This chapter will get you started with the benefits described below. **You can also call the Vets Hotline at 1-800-827-1000.**

Hospitalization Benefits

Nearly $7.5 billion is allotted annually nationwide for services provided by the Veterans Hospitalization Program. All veterans who received an honorable discharge are eligible for medical treatment and general healthcare that includes 80% coverage of all expenses. <u>In the case of hospitalization, any veteran is eligible for 100% hospital coverage at a VA hospital</u>, based on space available. Hospitalization includes neuropsychiatric care and related medical and dental services.

Dependents Program

The surviving children of deceased veterans are eligible for the CHAMP Plan, which provides medical care up to the age of 23. Surviving spouses are eligible for medical care until they remarry. The VA health plan does not cover dental work.

Prescription Service

Eligible veterans and certain dependents and survivors can receive prescription drugs and prosthetic medical supplies from VA pharmacies upon presenting prescriptions from licensed physicians. This program is open to veterans in treatment for service-connected conditions, or for conditions that required hospitalization and now require continued care on an outpatient basis. Other veterans may also be eligible. Contact your local VA Medical Center for details.

Nursing Home Care

For veterans who require skilled nursing care and related medical services for a long period of time, there is a Federal program under the VA especially designed for this purpose. To be eligible, you must have a VA hospital physician verify your need for long-term nursing care. Currently, this program provides home care services nationwide with an annual budget between $750 million and $1 billion. For more information, contact your local VA office or the VA Hotline at 1-800-827-1000.

Insider's Tip

The VA has also set aside funding to cover medical expenses for veterans in the treatment of mental disorders, both for hospitalization and outpatient care. Call the VA Hotline at 1-800-827-1000 for details.

Benefits for Disabled Veterans

The VA compensation program provides veterans with monthly benefits if they are disabled because of an injury or disease resulting from military service, or for certain conditions which developed after release from active duty. The amount of benefits is based upon the severity of the disabilities. If a veteran's service-connected disabilities are evaluated as 30% or more, additional benefits are available for their dependents. All veterans are eligible as long as they did not receive a dishonorable discharge.

There is no time limit to apply for VA disability compensation. However, the VA encourages veterans to apply within one year of their release because entitlement is retroactive to the date of leaving service, as long as the claim is filed within a one year.

How to Apply for Disability Benefits

Call the VA Hotline at 1-800-827-1000 and request VA Form 21-526. The following documents should be submitted along with the form:

• Service Medical Records—Applicants who have their service medical records are encouraged to submit them with their application to expedite processing. Otherwise, VA will contact the service department to obtain them.

• Other Medical Records — Medical records that show any and all treatment by private doctors and hospitals.

• Dependency Documents — Originals or copies of birth or marriage certificates and copies of divorce/death records relating to any prior marriages and those of your spouse.

• Military Discharge/DD Form 214 —Applicants who have a copy of their DD-214 are encouraged to provide a copy with their claim to expedite processing. Otherwise, VA will obtain verification from the service department.

More Disability Benefits

The VA also provides funding and/or services for disabled veterans in the following areas:

- Priority Inpatient and Outpatient Medical Care

- Prosthetics, Sensory and Rehabilitative Aids

- Clothing Allowance

- Automobile Grant

- Vocational Rehabilitation

- Disabled Veterans Life Insurance

- Preference for Employment in the Federal Government

- Job Finding Assistance

- Specially Adapted Housing Grant

- Dependents Educational Assistance Program

- Medical Care for Dependents and Survivors (CHAMPVA)

- Burial Benefits

- State and Local Benefits

Insider's Tip

At the state and local levels, grants are often available to pay the property taxes of veterans. To find out if your county has these grants available, call your local tax assessor or the VA Hotline at 1-800-827-1000.

Survivors' Benefits — Dependency and Indemnity Compensation (DIC)

DIC is a monthly cash benefit awarded to surviving spouses, unmarried children under 18, and helpless children or parents of veterans who die from service-connected causes. In some cases, entitlement can be established if the veteran's death is nonservice-connected.

A basic DIC payment is made monthly to eligible survivors. Additional amounts are available under special circumstances (e.g., for additional dependents or if a surviving spouse is severely disabled and in need of regular aid and attendance). Income does not affect DIC payments to surviving spouses and children; however, for eligible parents, the monthly DIC payment depends on the parent's income from other sources.

How To Apply for Survivor's Benefits

Call the VA Hotline at 1-800-827-1000 and ask for VA Form 21-534, Application for Dependency and Indemnity Compensation, Death Pension and Accrued benefits by a Surviving Spouse or Child (including Death compensation, if applicable). If you are a surviving parents, ask for VA Form 21-535, Application for Dependency and Indemnity Compensation by Parent(s).

Submit the following documents along with the application form:

• Dependency Documentation — Original or copy of birth and marriage certificates and copies of divorce/death records for all prior marriages of both veteran and spouse. Parents applying for DIC should furnish the original or a copy of the veteran's birth certificate.

• Military Discharge/DD Form 214 — Original or a certified copy. If this is not available, the VA will obtain verification from the service department.

• Certification of Death — Original or a copy of the veteran's death certificate.

Big Benefits for Veterans!

As you can see from this chapter, there are many exciting options for veterans medical benefits. Remember, if you served your country, you are entitled to these benefits—and the spouses, children, and parents of veterans are eligible as well. As we said at the beginning of this chapter, 1/3 of all Americans have the potential to qualify for medical assistance from the VA. Your own parents and even yourself may be eligible. For more information, call the VA Hotline today!

Chapter 17
The Viatical Option

Each and every day someone dies penniless because they were unaware that their life insurance policy could help them financially while they were still alive. Many people suffering from a terminal illness, and the financial burden that comes with it, don't know that a source of funds can be just a phone call away.

Anyone with a terminal illness who has a diagnosed life expectancy of four years of less, and who has a life insurance policy currently in effect, should consider contacting a viatical settlement company. Viatical settlement companies allow terminally ill patients to sell off all or part of their life insurance policies in exchange for an immediate cash amount. This can be a boon to very ill patients in the last days of their lives, given that terminal illness usually includes loss of employment and income, not to mention high medical costs.

Can Your Life Insurance Company Help?

Most whole life and universal life insurance policies accrue cash value after a few years. If you have owned one of these policies for many years, the cash value may be substantial. Cash value is the money you have already paid into the policy, plus interest, less the cost of insurance. Call your insurance company to find out what the cash value of your policy is and how to access it.

Your insurance company may offer an "accelerated" or "living benefit" on your whole life or universal life policy if you meet certain qualifications. Generally, the insurance company requires a maximum life expectancy of 6 months to one year, and then pays anywhere from 25% to 95% of the face value of the policy. Most insurance companies offer somewhere between 50% - 75%. Upon your death, the insurance company pays the remainder, less administrative fees, to your beneficiary/beneficiaries.

Viatical Settlement Companies: The Longer-Life Option

Viatical settlement companies offer alternatives for people with longer life expectancies than six months to 1 year, and in some cases, they will offer you more money than your insurance company. Viatical companies work with all types of policies, not just whole life and universal life. Group, individual, term and permanent insurance all qualify, provided that the policy is not subject to a suicide exclusion or contestability period (which usually applies to the policy's first two years).

Most viatical companies specialize in buying certain types of insurance policies. Some companies prefer to buy policies within a specific benefit range (for example, $25,000 to $150,000). Other companies deal with policies of $200,000 or more. Some prefer individual policies only, and some prefer policies for individuals with one year or less to live.

Because there are so many options, you may want to use a viatical settlement broker or consultant to assist you in the process. These brokers know which viatical companies buy what types of insurance policies, and many brokers will process your application with no fee to you. Viatical brokers can save you the time, energy and stress associated with seeking a viatical settlement.

All About Brokers

Viatical settlement brokers don't offer funding themselves—instead, they act as agents on behalf of terminally ill patients, in return for a percentage of the total cash settlement. Usually the broker takes 5% to 15% of the total.

Brokers deal not only with viatical funding companies, but also with private individuals and organizations who prefer that their involvement be kept confidential. Here are the advantages of dealing with a Viatical Settlement Broker:

• Brokers simplify what can be a highly complex process. Usually all they require is a single application form and physician's report.

• Brokers know which Funding Sources are most appropriate for a patient's cirumstances, and have access to funding sources that patients have no way of knowing about.

• Brokers are skilled at finding and negotiating the best terms of sale, so you get a higher settlement that more than covers the broker's commission.

Licensed Brokers vs. Non-Licensed

Viatical settlement brokers must meet state licensing requirements in eleven states: California, Florida, Louisiana, Minnesota, New York, North Carolina, Oregon, Texas, Vermont, Washington, and Wisconsin. In Illinois, Louisiana, Oregon, and Washington, brokers are not required to be licensed, but they must operate through an appointment from a Viatical Settlement Provider. In the states of Florida, Louisiana, and Washington, brokers must also be registered as a Life Agent.

In states that don't require licensing, there's no way to guarantee the reliability of viatical brokers or companies. Patients or their representatives should consult the Viatical Association of America for an updated list of approved Brokers and Funding Sources. The Viatical Association of America can also answer any questions you have about viatical settlements. Contact them at:

Viatical Association of America
1200 19th St., N.W.
Washington, D.C. 20036-2412
(202) 429-5129
FAX: (202) 429-5113

Insider's Tip:

A viatical settlement is a complicated financial transaction. It's always a good idea to speak with your attorney, accountant or financial advisor before proceeding.

Getting the Money

After applying for a viatical settlement through a broker, it usually takes from three to six weeks for the cash settlement to be paid—usually in the form of a cashier's check or wire transfer. And here's more good news:

with an established viatical settlement company, there is no penalty if the patient recovers or exceeds the estimated life expectancy!

Being Your Own Broker

If you are a skilled negotiator or have one who can go to bat for you, you can approach viatical companies through funding source organizations and save on the cost of the broker's fee. Funding source organizations offer settlements directly to terminally ill patients without using a broker or middleman.

You or your legal representative negotiate the terms of the settlement, based on your medical records, life expectancy, the size of the insurance policy, insurance company rating, amount of premium, and so on. Depending on these factors and your negotiating skill, the amount of the final settlement will range anywhere from 30% to 80% of the face value of your life insurance policy.

If you decide to pursue a viatical settlement on your own, it's recommended that you apply to three or four viatical settlement companies at the most. In addition to completing the paperwork for each company, you'll have to keep track of the process and negotiate the sale as well.

To cut the best deal, take your time and be persistant. Know that one or two more weeks of negotiating is probably worth the wait to get a bigger settlement. If you need the cash immediately, though, be prepared to take less for your policy.

Insider's Tip

When you submit an application to a viatical settlement company, be sure that the settlement amount you request is the exact amount you'll end up with. Check to see that no fees will be taken out at the end!

Important Questions to Ask Viatical Companies

- How long does the process take?

- How much can I expect to receive?

- Will there be extra costs to me?

- Will the offer I get be a net offer?

- What if I change my mind? Will I be under any obligation?

- Once I accept an offer, will the money go into an escrow account?

A Better Life

The important thing to remember about the viatical option is that it can give the chance for a better life to those who are living with a terminal illness. The value of your life insurance policy can work for you while you're still alive, and ease financial hardship for yourself and your loved ones. In the most difficult of times, it can be an option well worth looking into. You'll find a list of brokers and a list of viatical settlement companies at the end of this chapter.

Viatical Settlement Brokers

Benefit Advocates
599 Higuera St., Suite H
San Luis Obispo, CA 93401
(805) 541-8899
(800) 435-8891

Benefits America
3109 Maple Drive, Suite 404
Atlanta, GA 30305
(404) 233-5411
(800) 777-8878

Fiedler Financial
3030 Bridgeway, Suite 230
Sausalito, CA 94965
(415) 332-1444
(800) 905-0114

Individual Benefits, Inc.
7A Terrace Way
Greensboro, NC 27403
(910) 299-5100
(800) 800-3264

The Medical Escrow Society
205 North Texas Avenue, Suite 3
Tavares, FL 32778
(800) 422-1314

National Viator Representatives, Inc.
56 West 57th St.
New York, NY 10019
(212) 586-5600
(800) 932-0050

Viatical Funding Source Organizations

Accelerated Benefits Capital
25900 Greenfield Rd., Suite 230
Oak Park, MI 48237
(810) 967-4400
(800) 327-8222
(Additional offices in Chicago and
St. Louis)

AMG/Neuma, Inc.
8707 Skokie Blvd., Suite 230
Skokie, IL 60077
(847) 674-1150
(800) 457-7828

Legacy Benefits Corporation
225 West 34th St., Suite 1408
New York, NY 10122
(212) 643-1190
(800) 875-1000

Life Benefactors
124 University Ave.
San Diego, CA 92103
(619) 688-5920
(800) 285-5152
 (Additional offices in Houston,
Dallas, Philadelphia, Denver, Nashville,
Atlanta,San Francisco, Los Angeles,
and Palm Springs)

Life Time Benefits
The Pavillion
261 Old York Rd. #734
Jenkintown, PA 19046
(888) 300-5666
(215) 885-9100

LifeWise
136 S. Main St., Suite 700
The Kearns Building
Salt Lake City, UT 84101
(800) 219-7385

Portsmouth Financial Group, Inc.
One Georgia Center, Suite 510
Atlanta, GA 30308
(404) 876-2727
(800) 250-3230

ViatiCare Financial Services LLC
Hyatt Center
1300 Nicolett Mall, Suite 4060
Minneapolis, MN 55403-2609
(800) 333-2249

Viaticus, Inc.
200 South Wacker Dr., Suite 1400
Chicago, IL 60606
(800) 390-1390

Chapter 18
Service Organizations
and Foundations

D id you know that there are hundreds of charities, associations, foun dations and social service groups that provide FREE medical care and support nationwide? It's a fact—where Medicare and Medic- aid end, non-profit, private organizations begin, dispensing valuable free information, free counseling, free support groups, free gifts, and free goods and services—everything from free psychotherapy to groceries and money for bills or living expenses.

In this chapter we profile some of the national organizations that sup- ply free services and gifts. Please see *Free Cash Grants Volume 2* for more listings.

The Wellness Community

This nonprofit organization has a network of regional centers across the United States. This organization provides free psychotherapy and sup- port for anyone who asks. Best described as preventative health centers, The Wellness Community holds group and private therapy sessions for people living with various types of illness. For the Wellness Center branch nearest you, call their national office or one of the regional centers listed below.

NATIONAL OFFICE

The Wellness Community
10291 Reed Hartman Highway, Suite 215
Cincinnati, Ohio 45242
513-794-1116
Fax 513-794-1822

CALIFORNIA
Foothills
200 E. Del Mar Blvd., Suite 118
Pasadena, CA 91105
818-796-1083
Fax 818-796-0601

San Diego
8555 Aero Drive, #340
San Diego, CA 92123
619-467-1065
Fax 619-467-1082

San Francisco East Bay
1777 N. California Blvd., #200
Walnut Creek, CA 94596
510-933-0107
Fax 510-933-0249

South Bay Cities
109 W. Torrance Blvd., #100
Redondo Beach, CA 90277
310-376-3550
Fax 310-372-2094

Valley-Ventura
530 Hampshire Road
Westlake Village, CA 91361
805-379-4777
Fax 805-371-6231

West Los Angeles
2716 Ocean Park Blvd., Suite 1040
Santa Monica, CA 90405-5211
310-314-2555
Fax 310-314-7586

DELAWARE
1526 Gilpin Avenue
Wilmington, DE 19806
302-656-8410
Fax 302-656-5547

FLORIDA—SOUTHEAST
5700 N. Federal Highway
Boca Raton, FL 33487
561-912-9300
Fax 561-912-9301

FLORIDA—SOUTHWEST
3900 Clark Road, Bldg. P-3
Sarasota, FL 34233
941-921-5539
Fax 941-921-5061

GEORGIA
1776 Peachtree St., NW
Suite L-1
Atlanta, GA 30309
404-888-0050
Fax 404-888-0735

INDIANA—CENTRAL
8465 Keystone Crossing, #145
Indianapolis, IN 46240
317-257-1505
Fax 317-254-4534

MARYLAND
Dulaney Center II
901 Dulaney Valley Road, #710
Baltimore, MD 21204
410-832-2719
Fax 410-337-0937

MASSACHUSETTS
(Serves greater Boston area)
1320 Centre Street, #305
Newton Centre, MA 02159
617-332-1919
Fax 617-332-2727

MISSOURI
10425 Old Olive Street Road
St. Louis, MO 63141
314-993-4333
Fax 314-993-6835

OHIO
(Serves Greater Cincinnati-Northern Kentucky)
Bank One Towers
8044 Montgomery Road, #385
Cincinnati, OH 45236
513-791-4060
Fax 513-791-8239

PENNSYLVANIA
The Suzanne Morgan Center at
Ridgeland Mansion
Chamounix Dr., West Fairmount Park
Philadelphia, PA 19131
215-879-7733
Fax 215-879-6575

TENNESSEE
1844 Terrace Avenue
Knoxville, TN 37916
423-546-4661
Fax 423-522-1912

Ryan White Care Centers — AIDS & HIV Patients

The Ryan White Care Act, passed by the U.S. Congress in 1991, has set aside millions of dollars to be distributed to Ryan White Care Centers throughout the U.S. The Centers in turn provide AIDS and HIV sufferers with anything and everything it takes to stabilize their lives. Their services include counseling, free medical treatments (including prescription drugs), money for rent and utilities, and transportation to and from the doctor's office.

Ryan White Care Centers are staffed by individuals who work tirelessly toward helping their patients in every way. To locate the Care Center nearest you, call one of the following numbers:

National Association for People with AIDS — 1-800-838-9990

National AIDS Hotline — 1-800-342-AIDS

The Make-A-Wish Foundation of America

The Make-A-Wish Foundation grants wishes to any child between the ages of 2 1/2 and 18 who has a terminal illness or life-threatening medical condition. Make-A-Wish grants wishes to all eligible children regardless of race, religion or economic status. Today there are 82 chapters of The Make-A-Wish Foundation of America nationwide.

Volunteers from local chapters form "Wish Teams" that visit with the child and family and coordinate the wish. Although the most requested wish is to go to Disney World or Disneyland, the majority of wish requests fall into four major categories: "I want to go...; I want to be...; I want to meet...; or I want a...". There is absolutely no cost to the family. The average cost of granting a wish is $3,000 to $4,000.

Whenever possible, the family is included in the wish. For example, when Kathryn had been undergoing discouraging and painful treatments for leukemia, the Make-A-Wish Foundation fulfilled her dream of escaping to Hawaii. Along with wanting to experience the balmy weather, she had always wanted to swim and play with dolphins. Even though Kathryn lived with her family in Alaska where there is no Make-A-Wish chapter, the Washington State chapter sent Kathryn, her parents and her younger sister to Hawaii. There, under the guidance of experts, Kathryn coaxed a dolphin to roll over so she could rub its tummy. The patient mammal even allowed her to count its teeth! The Make-A-Wish Foundation gave Kathryn and her family a magical week away from hospitals and treatments where they could simply enjoy life.

Requests can be made by a parent, legal guardian, the child, or a medical professional. Requests should be directed to the chapter in your area. To locate the chapter nearest you, call the national office of the Make-A-Wish Foundation at 1-800-722-9474 and ask to speak to the chapter services department.

Ronald McDonald Houses

Ronald McDonald Houses is a national program with 182 houses nationwide. A Ronald McDonald House is a temporary "home away from home," where the families of children being treated for cancer and other serious illnesses live while the child receives treatment at a nearby hospital or medical treatment center. When a child receives outpatient therapy, the youngster can spend time with his family in the non-institutional atmosphere of the House.

This charity believes that sick children need more than quality medical attention. They need the emotional support and understanding of their parents, brothers and sisters. And families, in turn, need a place to stay where they can find stability when a child is seriously ill. For families forced to travel long distances to obtain medical care, their day-to-day problems are often compounded by lengthy separation from home and friends. They must often choose between paying for expensive hotels or sleeping in hospital waiting rooms to be close to their sick child.

At a Ronald McDonald House, the families have a place to rest, away from the institutional atmosphere of a hospital. Also, parents can share their worries and concerns with other parents and offer each other support during times of crisis.

Last year thousands of families were provided a comfortable, home-like environment near the places where their children were hospitalized. Families must apply through a local social services organization, since all applications are processed through social workers.

Camps for Kids

There are a number of free camps for children living with life-threatening illnesses. These, as well as other gift-giving charities, are listed in Appendix H of Free Cash Grants Volume II with addresses and phone numbers.

The Hole In the Wall Gang Summer Camps

Last year 1,000 seriously ill children with life-threatening diseases and blood disorders took part in camping programs, family weekends, retreats, circuses, and other programs through The Hole In the Wall Gang summer camps. Any child between the ages of 7 and 15 is eligible if a medical condition limits their physical activity and prevents them from enjoying traditional camp experiences. The counselor/staff ratio to camper is 2 to 1.

This is a national organization with camps in the New England states. Similar camping centers can be found in New York, Florida, and Illinois. The camp was started in 1987 by Paul Newman with profits from his company, Newman Foods. Since then, other organizations and individuals have continued to make donations of labor, money and goods. Today the 28-member board of directors raises $3.2 million for the annual budget. In 1996, The Hole in the Wall Gang Camp received the LEGO Group Award for outstanding humanitarian achievement.

Buffalo Prairie Gang

Affiliated with Paul Newman's The Hole in the Wall Gang Camps, the Buffalo Prairie Gang camps cover the Midwestern United States. By 1998 the camps in this region expect to provide a camping experience to 90 seriously ill children and their families per week all year round. The parents of seriously ill children between the ages of 6 and 15 should have their physician contact the organization on their behalf.

Double H Hole in the Woods Gang

This is another spin-off of Paul Newman's Hole in the Wall Gang Camps which serve seriously ill children and their families in the Northeastern United States. The campers are seriously ill children between the ages of 6 and 16 who have been diagnosed with cancer, blood disorders, HIV/AIDS, hemophilia, and conditions involving neuro-muscular impairment. Last year 900 children and their family members took part in camping programs, family weekends, and retreats.

The Boggy Creek Gang

The Boggy Creek Gang camps serve children in the Southeastern United States, primarily Florida. The campers are children between the ages of 7 and 15 who have cancer and related blood disorders, juvenile rheumatoid arthritis, sickle cell anemia, immunodeficiencies including HIV/AIDS, asthma, hemophilia, heart disease, and kidney disease.

Last year 1,200 children were given a full therapeutic summer camp experience, and 2,800 family members also took part in camping programs, family weekends, retreats, educational programs and sibling camps throughout the year.

Guide Dog Foundation for the Blind, Inc.

Last year this organization provided nearly 100 blind people with guide dogs. Eligible recipients were flown to the foundation's Smithtown, New York headquarters at no charge. For a period of 25 days, they were housed free of charge in dormitory quarters on the grounds. During that time they were given an intensive training program in the use, care, and handling of their guide dog — a trained companion given to them to assist in day-to-day living. Each dog is valued at $20,000, and they are FREE to eligible individuals.

Any legally blind person who is in good physical and mental health, is of adult age, and can adequately care for and house a guide dog is eligible. It should be noted that The Guide Dog Foundation's intention is that the prospective blind person is not a shut-in or a stay-at-home. If you would like to apply for a guide dog companion for yourself or family member or friend, call the Guide Dog Foundation for the Blind, Inc. at 1-800-548-4337.

Private Foundations

As we mentioned at the beginning of this section, $13 billion per year is given to U.S. residents for medical needs by private foundations. Some big corporations have set up charitable foundations for this purpose in their company's name. Due to the enormous tax benefits given to companies for setting up foundations, it's simply good business for them to set aside money for charitable purposes. Although some companies give grants only to their employees, the current trend among the Fortune 500 companies is to award grants on a national basis—Bigelow Tea, the Disney Corporation, and ITT, to name a few. See Appendix H in *Free Cash Grants Vol. 2* for a list of private, corporate, and community foundations.

There are also many other foundations that set aside millions of dollars per year for grants-in-aid. Some of the eligibility requirements for these grants are very specific—for example, the grant might specify that you need to be of German ancestry and live in the San Francisco Bay Area. Other foundations have eligibility requirements that are far more general, such as merely needing to be under 21 years of age and economically disadvantaged in order to receive free medical and dental care.

The only trick to being awarded a grant is to make sure that you meet the eligibility requirements. Doing so will dramatically increase your chances of getting the funding or services you need to live a better life. In the meantime, make it your goal to contact every social service agency and support group that relates to your condition.

Other Sources

The organizations we've described above are just a few of the charities dedicated to providing free services and gifts to the disabled and physically ill. There are many more similar organizations at the regional and local level. You can find them by making a quick trip to your local library, which will have a list of local foundations and associations. Nearly every community has a network of private charities that are dedicated to serving people with medical needs. Rest assured that they are out there, ready and willing to help you!

Checklist for the Successful Grant Seeker

Through our research we've discovered that individuals applying for grants are most successful when they follow these steps:

- Clearly identify your needs.

- Think of applying for grants as a part-time job.

- Gather all the necessary documents, i.e. tax returns, birth certificates, bank statements, health records, etc.

- Have multiple copies of these documents available to send with your grant applications.

- Set aside a small area for your grants paperwork and files.

- Write a letter of introduction and an explanation of your needs that can be used over and over.

- Ask everyone you know for help in finding the right agency, foundation, or corporation.

- Follow up on every lead.

- Be willing to spend whatever time it takes to complete these steps.

- Refuse to give up until you've achieved your goal!

Conclusion

By reading this book, you already know more than most Americans about free cash grants. Now that you have all the resources you need to get started, the only thing left to do is to begin! Don't hesitate—the sooner you apply for these grants, the closer you will be to living a new and better life!

For best results, use *Free Cash Grants Vols. 1 and 2* together . Volume 1 has the how-to; Volume 2 has the lists of actual grants. Together they form a great system for breaking into the world of grants. With everything you've got going for you, you're bound to be a winner!

Clarendon's Grant Program: Your Key to Success

With so many grants available from Federal, State, and private sources, we know that you may need some extra help to navigate the waters! Our Customer Assistance Group is standing by to answer your questions. Call 1-800-258-3770 Monday through Friday between the hours of 5 am and 6 pm PST (or Saturdays 7 am - 1 pm PST) for FREE assistance with all your grants questions.

At Clarendon, our business is based on building long-term relationships with customers to help them achieve their goals. So if you really want to find free cash grants, whether for your education, your business, or for medical expenses, we can help your dream come true! All it takes is a little know-how and persistence, and you could have the next success story we print in these pages!

Let Us Hear From You!

We are always seeking to improve the quality of the information included in this volume. If you have suggestions, comments, or success stories to share with us, let us hear from you! Simply send to: Success Stories, Clarendon House, Inc., 1919 State Street, Suite 112, Santa Barbara, CA 93101, Attention Rebecca Harris. To show you our appreciation, we'll send you a FREE publication that will be of GREAT INTEREST to you!

Index

NOTES

NOTES